MYSTIFYING

CARD TRICKS

BOB LONGE

Sterling Publis

New

STERLING Books by Bob Longe

101 Amazing Card Tricks
Easy Card Tricks
Easy Magic Tricks
Great Card Tricks
Mind Reading Magic Tricks
Nutty Challenges & Zany Dares
World's Best Card Tricks
World's Best Coin Tricks
World's Greatest Card Tricks

Library of Congress Cataloging-in-Publication Data

Longe, Bob, 1928–
  Mystifying card tricks / Bob Longe.
      p.   cm.
  Includes index.
  ISBN 0-8069-9454-1
  1. Card tricks I. Title
  GV1549.L529   1997
  795.4'38--dc20   96-35887
                                          CIP

2   4   6   8   10   9   7   5   3   1

Published in 2005 by Sterling Publishing Co., Inc.
387 Park Avenue South, New York, NY 10016
© 1997 by Bob Longe
Distributed in Canada by Sterling Publishing
℅ Canadian Manda Group, 165 Dufferin Street,
Toronto, Ontario, Canada M6K 3H6
Distributed in Great Britain and Europe by Chris Lloyd at Orca Book
Services, Stanley House, Fleets Lane, Poole BH15 3AJ, England
Distributed in Australia by Capricorn Link (Australia) Pty. Ltd.
P.O. Box 704, Windsor, NSW 2756, Australia

Sterling ISBN 1-4027-2457-8

For information about custom editions, special sales, premium and
corporate purchases, please contact Sterling Special Sales
Department at 800-805-5489 or specialsales@sterlingpub.com.

CONTENTS

Power of the Mind   95

Mind-Boggling Fun   114

The Threatening Kings   120

Mastery Levels Chart & Index   127

INTRODUCTION

An argument can be made that almost every calling requires some amount of selling. It's certainly true of such diverse occupations as teaching, medicine, journalism, law. And it's especially true of the performance of magic. The tricks are your product; the performance is selling.

A sales representative doesn't simply run the vacuum cleaner and expect a sale; he explains the benefits, indicates how much easier life will be, paints a picture of total cleanliness accomplished with ease. And with magic, you don't just perform a trick and hope for the best: You must sell the trick. Some magicians, particularly stage performers, accomplish this with props, music, costumes, and such. Even so, in most instances the principal selling tool is the voice.

This is certainly true of card tricks. Apart from the deck itself, what other tools do you have? So you should use your voice cleverly and thoughtfully. What are you trying to sell? Yourself, of course. The group should feel that you're a good person. If you are, this should be an easy sell. So let's not worry about that. Basically, then, you're trying to sell the spectators on the validity of the trick you're doing. In other words, you're trying to fool them. And, at the same time, you want to entertain them. Your patter, your demeanor, your entire presentation should be aimed at this dual goal.

So try to develop patter for each trick. Give it a lot of thought. Present a story that's either serious or amusing, but is always interesting. Perhaps include an anecdote or two. (If you tell a joke and people laugh, that's a joke. If you tell a joke and nobody laughs, that's an illustrative anecdote.) You can orally create an atmosphere of mystery, recount a tale that will misdirect the attention of the group, or make a series of silly remarks that evoke laughter. The possibilities are endless.

As you practice a trick, be sure to include the patter. Thus your patter will improve as you perfect the mechanics, and you'll end up with a perfectly integrated and entertaining trick.

In this book you'll find a fascinating collection of card tricks that especially lend themselves to patter, for you're involved in all sorts of mental magic: prediction, strange coincidence, telepathy, feats of the conscious mind, and a number of hilarious mental tricks. Patter themes should readily spring to mind. If they don't, however, I offer patter suggestions for almost every trick.

When you decide to do mental magic with cards, you must decide whether you're going to be serious about it or not. Are you going to purport that you have superior mental powers? I prefer to be just as baffled as the rest of the group, taking the attitude, "I don't know why it works; it just does." I figure that I'm just doing card tricks; why would I want to pretend that I have some sort of mysterious access to the ultimate powers of the universe?

A deck of cards is ideal for performing mental magic because so much variety is possible. In fact, using some of the tricks presented here, you can do an entire show of mental magic. Or—my preference—you can include several as a part of your regular program.

If you prefer not to do mental magic, you may perform many of these items as simply mystifying card tricks. The only difference is the patter.

I'm very proud of this collection, and I'm sure you'll find many tricks that you'll enjoy performing.

Note

For clarity, in many of the illustrations I have simplified the face of the cards, prominently displaying in the middle what would ordinarily be found at the corner (refer to Illus. 1, page 17).

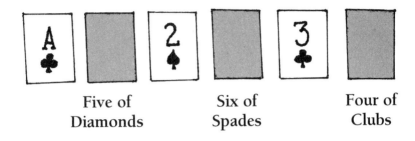

Five of   **Six of**   **Four of**
Diamonds   **Spades**   **Clubs**

Illus. 1

If the five of diamonds is chosen, you will turn over the other face-down cards. All the cards are now face up except for the five of diamonds. You point out that all the other cards are black. Turn over the five of diamonds; it's the only red-faced card.

If the two of spades is chosen, you will turn over the other face-up cards. All the cards are now face down except for the two of spades. You point out that all the other cards have blue backs. Turn over the two of spades; it's the only red-backed card.

Thus, it *appears* that the spectator chose the only card that's different from the others. Now let's see how precisely we arrive at this delightful conclusion.

Prior to your performance, set up the cards so that on top is the only red-faced card—in our example, the five of diamonds. Second from the bottom is the only red-backed card—in our example, the two of spades. (In our example, the setup, from top to bottom, will be five of diamonds, six of spades, four of clubs, three of clubs, two of spades, ace of clubs.)

In performance, get the assistance of Albert, who—poor boy!—actually thinks he has some degree of psychic ability.

"I'd like you to assist me in an experiment, Albert." Take the packet from your envelope, or wallet, or pocket. "I have six cards here. I'll send you a psychic message and see if you receive it."

Turn the packet face up and hold it in the left hand in the dealing position (Illus. 2).

Illus. 2

In the illustration, the card at the face of the packet is the ace of clubs. Deal this card face up to your left. About four inches to the right of this, deal the next card (two of spades) face up. And, about four inches to the right of this, deal the next card (three of clubs) face up (Illus. 3).

Illus. 3

Turn the remai
ing the packet fac
tion. Deal the top
first space on you
of clubs and two
face down into t
spades and three
face down on th
that was original

three-card packet over. You're now hold-
wn in your left hand in the dealing posi-
l (five of diamonds) face down into the
—in other words, between the face-up ace
ades. The next card (six of spades) goes
.t space to the right, between the two of
bs. And the last card (four of clubs) goes
t end. The cards are now in the position
wn in Illus. 1.

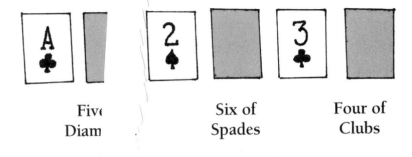

Fiv(Six of   Four of
Diam   Spades   Clubs

Original positions

"Six cards
message." W
Albert gets th
between one
mind, so tha
have a num
He does.
end."
Because
numbers tv
end up wi
(Take a loo

lbert, and I'm going to send you a psychic
gers to temples, concentrate, hoping that
sage. "Now, Albert, please think of a number
ix. After you've thought of one, change your
know that this is not psychological. Do you
ween one and six?"
ie the number, and we'll count it from the

d "between one and six," he is confined to
, four, or five. This means that Albert will
the second or third card from your left.
riginal positions again, shown above.)

If he gives the number two or five, he will end up with the second card from your left. Say he gives the number two. Start with the card on the left end and count one, two—ending on the second card from your left. If he gives the number five, start with the card on the right end and count one, two, three, four, five—again ending on the second card from your left. In either instance, push the "chosen" card forward about an inch or so (Illus. 4).

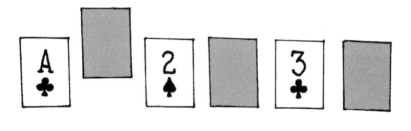

Illus. 4

Turn the other face-down cards face up (Illus. 5). "Notice that all the others are black cards."

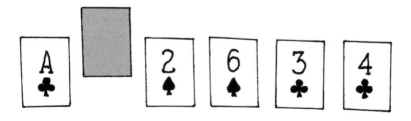

Illus. 5

'   ) that the cards are ordinary in every way." After fan-
nin   al cards into your right hand, place these on top of
the

F   )ugh several more and place these on top also.
Con   )ing this until you come to the six of clubs, which
you   ιo the right hand below the others that you have
alrea   ned over. Place this group on top of the deck. The
six o   is now on top of the deck. Fan out several more
cards   /er. Then close up the deck, turn it face down, and
set it   table in front of Spectator 1.

Tak   deck from Spectator 2 and go through the precise
same |ure as you did with the other deck. Set the deck
on the   in front of Spectator 2. The six of clubs, of course,
is the t   ırd.

"No |ould like each of you to pick up your deck. Please
cut off   ιll packet of cards from the top, turn the packet
over, ar   ce it back on top of the deck." When they're done,
continu   ıxt, cut off a larger packet from the top of the deck,
turn this   ket over, and place it back on top of the deck."

Make   ؟ they are following your instructions exactly.
"Please,   of you fan off the face-up cards and set them
down or   table. The next card in your pile will be your chosen card.   please don't look at it just yet."

Why   :dn't they look at it immediately? One reason is
that you   t to build suspense. But more important, you
want to   ؟veryone a chance to forget exactly what happened. Th   called "time misdirection." Given a chance, many
spectators   forget that you even handled the cards, or that
you carefu   rected the choice of a card.

"Each o   assistants has selected a card completely at random. I do   that anyone here could, with any confidence,
name eith   ιosen card. And don't forget that we have a
newspaper   here, and that I took out a significant ad in it."
Or, the last   ؟ence might be, "And don't forget that I wrote
something   ι on a slip of paper which has been in plain
sight from t   ginning."

Ask Spectator 1 to turn over the top card of those remaining in his hand. "What's the name of your card, please?"

He names it—the six of clubs. Do the same thing with Spectator 2. Unbelievably, they both have selected the same card! And, even more incredibly, you have predicted their choice with an ad or by jotting the name on a slip of paper.

Note

If it doesn't strike you as too much trouble, you could use new, unopened decks. Unless you're doing a platform presentation, I think this might be a bit cumbersome, however. At someone's home, I highly recommend that, if possible, you borrow the two decks.

Simple Multiplication

Of the general public, hardly anyone is familiar with this mathematical peculiarity: The number 142,857, when multiplied by 2, 3, 4, 5, or 6, will yield precisely the same digits that make up the original number. (In fact, the digits remain in the same basic order, which is not relevant in this trick.)

Some rudimentary tricks have been fashioned from this principle. It seemed to me, however, that an excellent mental trick could be created. This one works quite well for me.

The only thing you need remember is the number I mentioned: 142,857. I use this mnemonic:

Unfortunate 57. (57, as in 57 varieties.) For purposes of the mnemonic, I pronounce "unfortunate" like this:

$$
\begin{array}{ll}
\textbf{un-} & \textbf{(1)} \\
\textbf{for-} & \textbf{(4)} \\
\textbf{tune-} & \textbf{(2)} \\
\textbf{ate.} & \textbf{(8)}
\end{array}
$$

So you get 1 (an ace), 4, 2, 8—and then 57 (varieties). As you can see, *142,857* is your key number.

To begin, ask George to assist you.

Fan through the deck, faces toward yourself, and remove cards that match your key number—except for the first digit. In other words, remove from the deck and place face down onto the table cards of these values:

4 2 8 5 7

"These are my prediction cards, George. If all goes well, some of these will match cards which you will choose completely by chance."

Once more fan through the deck. This time, remove cards that will match the entire key number. As you remove them, lay them out in their proper order, muttering, "We'll need a variety of cards. These ought to do" (Illus. 14.).

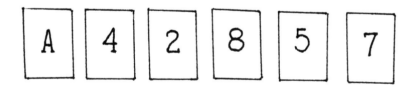

Illus. 14

George should be side-by-side with you.

"Here we have six cards, George. I'd like you to choose a number to multiply these by. We'll have to select a number completely by chance. So I'd like you to mentally throw a die. If you throw a one, please mentally toss it again, because one simply duplicates the values we have here. We'll need a two, three, four, five, or six. Now mentally throw that die."

George does so.

"What number did you get?"

He tells you. Suppose he says five. Fan through the deck and remove a five, placing it below the other cards, as shown in Illus. 15.

Illus. 15

"Now let's do the multiplication together."

You proceed to multiply the number by five. "Five times seven is 35," you say. "Put down the five, and carry the three." Fan through the deck and find a five; place it below the other cards (Illus. 16).

"Five times five is 25," you continue. "Add the three that we carried, and we have 28. So we put down the eight, and carry the two."

Look through the deck and find an eight. Place it to the left of the five that you placed down (Illus. 17).

| A | 4 | 2 | 8 | 5 | 7 |

| | | | | | 5 |

| | | | | | 5 |

Illus. 16

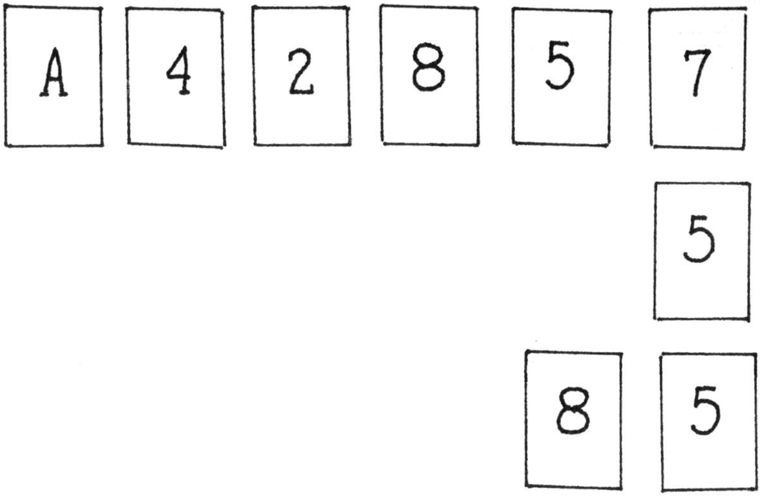

| A | 4 | 2 | 8 | 5 | 7 |

| | | | | | 5 |

| | | | | 8 | 5 |

Illus. 17

Continue until you complete the entire multiplication process (Illus. 18). In this instance you end up with 714285.

"Is my multiplication correct, George?" It is.

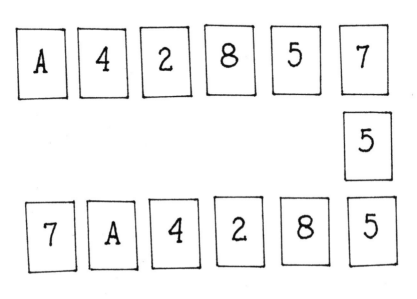

Illus. 18

Gather up all the cards that were used in the calculation except for the answer. Turn these face down and place them on top of the deck.

Casually shuffle the cards as you say, "George, please gather up the cards that we arrived at through multiplying by your number. Hold them as you might hold a bridge hand. Sometimes I'm very lucky at bridge. Let's see if that works out here. How many cards do you have?"

He has six cards.

"Oh, you should have five. Let's see . . . we'll eliminate the highest card. I can't remember, what is your highest card . . . a nine?" Eventually, you'll discover that it's an ace. Have him hand it to you. Place it on top of the deck and set the deck aside.

Pick up your prediction pile and hold it the same way that you would hold a bridge hand.

"We each have a five-card hand, George. We'll find out if I'm lucky or not. You arrived at your cards by multiplying some cards by a freely selected number. Let's see if my prediction matches any of your cards. Place one of your cards face up on the table."

He does. "Oh, good! I have one of those." Place the matching card face up on top of his card.

"Let's try another."

He places another one of his cards either face up in another spot on the table, or on top of the other two cards. Either way, you match it.

Continue through the other three cards.

Note

You eliminate the ace from the final revelation because it's the most obvious card in the deck and could possibly tip off the method.

Slick Sticker Trick

Master magician Ron Bauer showed me the original trick, which is extremely strong. The only problem is that a bit of preparation is involved and that the performer must be sitting down with a spectator sitting opposite him.

I have come up with four variations which have fewer restrictions. However, you will need a pen. Also, all versions of the trick require the use of those little reminder stickers, ones that are one and a half by two inches in size. A portion of one side has a sticky substance on it for temporarily attaching the paper to something. The product is available at most stores that carry office supplies.

The Original Trick

Here is the trick that Ron showed me:

You're sitting at a table quite close, with your legs well under the table. Unknown to the group, you have a playing card face down on your lap. On the back of the card is a sticker. Let's say that the card in your lap with the blank sticker is the six of spades.

A group may be gathered around you, but sitting opposite you is Hedda, the person for whom you're performing the trick. Have her shuffle the deck.

Take the deck back and explain, "Hedda, in a moment I'm going to ask you to choose a card. But I'm going to ask you to do it *under the table*, so that the choice will be completely by chance. So I'll hand you the deck *face up* under the table, and I'd like you to cut off a portion and turn it over, like this."

Demonstrate by holding the deck face up in your left hand. Cut off some cards with your right hand and turn them face down on top of the others. Make sure that Hedda understands. Restore the cards to their original order.

You're now holding the deck face up in your left hand. Take a sticker and affix it to the bottom card, precisely the way the sticker is affixed to the six of spades on your lap.

"Hedda, I'm going to write a prediction on the sticker, but I don't want you to see it just yet." Tilt the cards up so that Hedda cannot see the bottom card. With your pen print this on the sticker: 6S (shorthand for six of spades), as shown in Illus. 19.

It doesn't really matter if others see what you print on the sticker.

"Now I'll hand you the cards under the table. And while the cards are still under the table, I want you to cut off a portion and turn it over, just as I showed you."

As you near the end of your little speech, place the deck face up under the table with both hands. With your right hand, pick up the face-down six of spades and place it, as is, at the face of the deck. Immediately, reach your right hand forward, apparently searching for Hedda's hand.

"Now where's your hand? Ah, here we go."

The situation: You're holding the deck face up in your left hand. On top of the face-up deck is one face-down card, the six of spades. On the back of the six of spades is a blank sticker. Just below the six of spades is the first of the face-up cards. On its face is a sticker with "6S" printed on it.

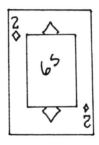

Illus. 19

With your right hand, you've located Hedda's hand. With your left hand, give the deck to Hedda. Bring both hands out from under the table.

In all likelihood, Hedda will feel the sticker on the uppermost card. By no means, mention this!

Just tell her, "When you're done cutting and turning the packet over on top, just bring the cards out."

When she's done, take the cards from her and spread them out onto the table. The uppermost cards will be face down.

Spread out the face-down cards to the point where the face-up cards begin. The first of these will be the six of spades that you added under the table (Illus. 20).

Illus. 20

The card facing it has the prediction sticker on its face. Point to the six of spades, saying, "Here's the card you cut to—the six of spades. Now let's take a look at my prediction." Turn over the card facing it—the last of the face-down cards—revealing your prediction: 6S!

The trick is over. But, if you're going to do more tricks, you must get rid of the sticker on the back of the six of spades. The best bet, I believe, is to have a duplicate deck of cards in a card case in your pocket. Take the sticker off your prediction card; then gather up all of the cards, put them into their card case, and place the case into your pocket. If the group wants more magic, remove the duplicate deck from your pocket and proceed.

Variations
I have four more versions of the trick. All are effective, but each has its strengths and its weaknesses. In all of them, the person

for whom you're performing (Hedda) must be seated at a table, but you need not be.

Version 1: This is my favorite.

Again, there is a bit of preparation. Place a sticker on the back of a card. Put this card on the bottom of the deck.

Take out the deck and fan through the cards face down, not quite to the bottom. As you do this, say, "In a moment, I'm going to ask you to select one of these cards, Hedda." (You *don't* want to say anything like, "An ordinary deck of cards," or, "Notice that I haven't put a sticker on the back of any cards.")

Turn the deck face up and fan through several cards from the face of the deck. Note the second card from the bottom; this is your prediction card. Again, let's assume that it's the six of spades.

As you fan through the cards, say, "You'll choose any card you wish." Even the cards up and continue. "But first, I'm going to make a prediction. Then I want you to take the deck, cut off a portion, and turn it over like this." Pick up about half and turn the packet over, but don't set it completely down. "Okay?" Return the deck to its original face-up position. The card at the face has a blank sticker on the back. The card below it is the six of spades.

As before, place a sticker on the face of the bottom card and print your prediction, 6S. With both hands, take the deck under the table. Turn the uppermost card over.

The situation: The card at the face of the deck now has the blank sticker uppermost; below this card is the six of spades. In exactly the same manner as before, give Hedda the deck.

She cuts the cards as directed and brings the deck out. Have her set it on the table.

A bit of "time misdirection" is vital here. So you say something like this: "I had no way of knowing where you'd cut the cards. Yet I had the gall to make a prediction. And if that prediction should work out, it'll prove that I have the ability to foresee the future. Or not."

Spread the cards out onto the table. The top group, of course, consists of face-down cards. The first face-up card has a prediction on its face: 6S. Point this out. Then turn over the last face-down card, showing that it's the six of spades.

As in the first version, you must get rid of the extra sticker if you plan to do more tricks.

The reason for the "time misdirection" is that the relative positions of the "sticker" card and the predicted card are illogical; actually, the two should be exchanged. So far, no one has noticed.

Version 2: This one requires no preparation, and you end up with nothing to get rid of.

Have Hedda shuffle the deck. You fan through the cards, both face down and face up, saying, "Hedda, you'll be able to choose any one of these cards that you wish." As you fan through the face-up cards, note the third card from the bottom; this is the card you'll predict. Again, let's assume it's the six of spades.

Go through the explanation of how a pile is to be cut off and turned over onto the other cards.

Hold the cards face up, saying, "I'll make a prediction now." Call attention to the bottom card. Let's suppose it's the five of diamonds. Turn it over so that it's face down on top of the face-up cards. Put a sticker on it. Tilt the cards up so that Hedda can't see what you print. As always, print 6S on the sticker. This time, you turn the card over again, so that the sticker doesn't show. Explain to Hedda, "I don't want you to see the prediction yet."

Hand the cards to Hedda beneath the table in the usual manner. This time, however, you turn over the two uppermost cards together before handing the deck over.

The situation: Uppermost is a face-down card (of no significance). Below it is the face-down five of diamonds, with a sticker on the back; the sticker is marked 6S. Below this card is the first face-up card, the six of spades.

Hedda performs the cut as directed and brings the deck forth. Again, she sets it onto the table. Since the two critical cards will not be in their logical positions, you again use some "time misdirection."

Then you spread the cards out onto the table. You turn over the last face-down card, showing that it's the six of spades. Call attention to the first face-up card, the five of diamonds. Turn it over and show your prediction.

You're all set to perform more tricks. *But* you've lost the feature in which the spectator can feel the sticker on the card.

Version 3: Here, the second card from the bottom has a blank sticker on its back.

You start by fanning through the face-down cards, almost to the bottom. And then fan through the face-up cards, noting the third card from the bottom—as usual, the six of spades.

You explain how to cut the cards.

A sticker is placed on the face of the bottom card. You tilt the deck toward yourself and print 6S on the sticker.

As in the previous version, you turn over the uppermost two cards together before handing Hedda the deck. When Hedda brings the deck out, you again use "time misdirection."

When you spread the deck out, you fan through to the first face-up card, which shows your prediction. And you show the last face-down card, which is the card you predicted (the six of spades).

The advantage is that the spectator feels the sticker; the disadvantage is that you must get rid of the extra sticker.

Version 4: In some respects, this is the best version of the bunch: There is no setup, the position of the critical cards is logical, and there's no cleanup. But you lose the advantage of the spectator feeling the sticker.

The deck is shuffled by Hedda. You take the deck back, saying, "Hedda, you'll have complete freedom in choosing any one of these cards." You hold the deck face down and rapidly fan through about a quarter of the deck. Close up the deck and turn it face up. Fan through about a quarter of the deck again. As you do so, note and remember the bottom card. Let's say it's the six of spades.

Turn the deck *face down*. Demonstrate how Hedda is supposed to take the face-down cards, cut off a portion, turn it over, and place it on top of the other cards.

Turn the top card face up and put a sticker on it. In the usual way, make your prediction—print 6S. Turn the card face down.

Before handing Hedda the deck under the table, slip the bottom card to the top, turning it face up in the process.

When Hedda brings the deck out, the top portion is face up and the bottom portion face down. You spread the cards out onto the table. The last face-up card contains your prediction on its face—just as it should. And the first face-down card is the six of spades, your prediction card.

Note

I understand that this trick is derived from one in which stickers were not used—the prediction was made on a card with a marking pen. This can be very effective, if you don't mind losing a card now and then. See how this method might work out with some of my variations, particularly with the last version, Number 4.

COINCIDENCE OR UNEXPLAINABLE CONCURRENCE

Lucky in Love

This trick is calculated to make everyone feel good, particularly the person who volunteers to assist you.

A bit of preparation is necessary. Take any nine black cards from the deck and place them on top. On top of these, put the queen of hearts.

Jim is a bachelor with no particular attachment to a young lady, so he would be the perfect choice to assist you.

Once you have enlisted Jim's help, casually fan off ten cards from the top of the deck and hand them to him, saying, "We'll just need a small packet of cards."

You should keep the cards in the same order. This can be easily done by counting the cards in groups of three as you fan them out, taking them—one under the other—into the right hand.

"Jim, we want to find out whether you'll be lucky in love. So I'd like you to think of a number that you really like—some number from, say, one to ten. It could be a lucky number, a number that has some significance in your life, or—if all else fails—a number that simply occurs to you."

Continue, "Do you have your number? Good. Now I'll turn my back and I'd like you to transfer that many cards, one at a time, from the top to the bottom of your packet. For instance, if your number were three, you'd move three cards one at a time to the bottom of your packet."

Turn away. When you turn back, take the packet from Jim, saying, "We'd better mix these a bit." Transfer ten cards from the top to the bottom of the packet, using the *One–Two–Three Shift*, described starting on page 7. This, of course, keeps the packet in the same order.

Deal the top card face down onto the table to the right. On top of it, and overlapping to the right, deal the next card. The third card also overlaps to the right. Continue until the entire packet is dealt out. (Illus. 21 is from your point of view.) Perform this deal fairly rapidly and, as you do so, say, "So here's your packet."

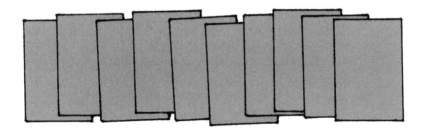

Illus. 21

A bit of "time misdirection" would be appropriate here.

"Obviously, Jim, I have no way of knowing what number you chose. As we all know, it could be any number from one to ten. So now I'd like you to use that number to select a card. Just count to that number in this packet." As you utter the last sentence, start at your right side of the spread, touching first the top card of the bunch, then the second card, and finally the third card. This shows him precisely how he is to count.

If Jim counts to his card aloud, fine. But if he counts silently, mentally count along with him. Suppose he stops with his finger resting on the seventh card. You make sure he got it right by saying, "So you thought of the number seven, right?"

Have him slide his selection away from the other cards. "But don't look at your card just yet. Let's see what you might have picked."

Turn over all the other cards. All of them are black. "You could have chosen one of these very negative cards. So let's see what you picked."

He turns over the queen of hearts.

"The queen of hearts! The symbol of love. Jim, you're really going to be lucky in love."

Notes

(1) The trick may done in exactly the same way for a woman.

(2) If your assistant is in a happy relationship with a person of the opposite sex, you simply change the wording at the beginning: "We want to find out if you *are* lucky in love."

Three-Card Coincidence

I believe Martin Gardner invented this trick and that Nick Trost developed what I consider a stronger version. I have added a slight twist to the Trost trick.

Remove from the deck the ace, two, and three of clubs, hearts, and diamonds. As you take them from the deck, toss them face up onto the table. Set the rest of the deck aside.

Nora believes in ESP, for all you know, so ask her to assist you.

"If we both concentrate, Nora, this experiment is sure to work. In fact, if we both have the proper attitude this should be as easy as one, two, three. That's why I have three sets of 'one-two-three' right here on the table."

Go through the cards on the table and form three face-up groups, each consisting of an ace, a two, and a three. Each set of three should include a club, a heart, and a diamond. *Make sure the cards are spread out so that you can tell the order of the suits.* Let's say that the three groups are those shown in Illus. 22.

Group 1

Group 2

Group 3

Illus. 22

Address Nora, "Please select one of the groups of three for yourself. Just pick up one of the groups."

Let's say she picks up Group 1.

"Good. Now which group should we leave on the table face up?"

We'll assume that she selects Group 2. Pick up Group 2. Before proceeding, look at the remaining group and note the order of the suits from the bottom up. In this instance, you note that the order of suits in Group 3 is clubs, diamonds, hearts. Deal Group 2 into a face-up row so that, from left to right, the suits are in the same order as Group 3 (Illus. 23).

Illus. 23

Pick up Group 3 and hold it face down.

The situation: We have three groups of cards consisting of ace, two, and three of different suits. Nora is holding Group 1. Face up in a row on the table is Group 2. You're holding Group 3. Your top card matches the suit of Group 2's card on the left. Your second card matches the suit of Group 2's middle card. And your bottom card matches the suit of Group 2's card on the right.

"Apparently, I get this group, Nora. I'll put them down here."

Deal your three cards in a face-down row aligned just below Group 2 (Illus. 24).

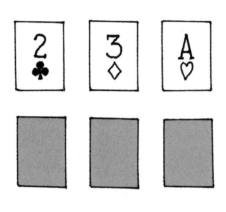

Illus. 24

"It's your turn, Nora. Without letting me see any cards, I'd like you to put your cards face down in a row right here." Indicate a spot above Group 2. "When you put your cards down, make sure you don't match any of the face-up cards in value. In other words, don't put a two below a two."

When she finishes, say, "I already know you did a perfect job." Turn each of the Group 2 cards face down in place, saying, "We'll forget these."

Point to her cards. "Put your hand on one of your cards. I'll touch my matching card—the card in the same column. We'll turn them over together and see how we match up."

There are now two possible endings:

Ending 1: Nora and you turn over two corresponding cards. They are of the same value.

"They match!" you shriek. Place your card face up on top of her face-up card. Again you turn over two corresponding cards, and again they match in value. And, of course, the remaining two also match in value.

Ending 2: Nora and you turn over two corresponding cards. They are of the same *suit*. You are far more excited about this than she is.

"Look at that!" you declare, utterly astounded. "They're both the same suit." Place your card face up on top of her face-up card. You go through the procedure twice more, matching the suit each time.

"I wonder if it's possible that . . . Let's see." Turn over Group 3's card on the left. It's the same suit as the others in its column. Place it face up on top of the other two cards. "Ah, a perfect group of three!"

Do the same with the middle card of Group 3 and then the card on the right. All three cards in each column are of the same suit.

With either ending, you have quite a coincidence.

Lucky Numbers

This is my version of a Peter Wilker trick in which he used an old principle to fashion an astonishing mental trick. Beforehand, take the two red queens from the deck. Place one on top of the deck and one on the bottom.

Jenny enjoys a good card trick, so she'll probably be happy to help you out. Set the deck onto the table and say, "Jenny, would you please cut off about half the cards and place them onto the table next to the others."

After she does this, pick up the original lower portion of the deck, saying, "Let's see how close you came to half." Count the cards aloud as you take them one on top of the other. (If you prefer, you can count them into a pile on the table.) Whatever number you end up with, say, "That's amazing. You just gave them a casual cut, and you came extremely close to cutting them exactly in half. Now I know this experiment is going to work."

At this point a red queen is on top of each pile.

Place the piles side by side. "In magic, Jenny, there are two really significant numbers—seven and 13. We're going to use both of them in this experiment. Let's start with seven. Please give me any number from one to seven."

Suppose she chooses four. Counting aloud, you deal four cards simultaneously from each pile, placing each card face down next to its pile. In other words, you deal to the right of the pile on the right, and to the left of the pile on the left.

Turn over the top card of each of the piles you dealt off. Usually, the cards will be quite different in suit and value. Comment on their differences.

If their suits or colors happen to be the same, mention, "Good! That's a start."

If the cards happen to be of the same value, say, "This is amazing. Four must be your lucky number."

Turn the two cards face down and replace them on the dealt-off piles. Place the dealt-off piles back onto their original piles. "Now, Jenny, let's try the number 13. Please give me any number higher than seven but not more than 13."

Let's say she chooses 11. As before, deal off that number to the side of each pile. Again show the top card of each pile you dealt off. Comment on the cards, calling attention to their similarities and differences. Replace these cards face down on top of their respective counted-off piles. Place the counted-off piles back onto their original piles.

"So far," you say, "we haven't accomplished much. But let's see if your two chosen numbers have *combined* power. Your numbers were four and 11. So we'll start with four."

As before, you simultaneously deal the cards to the side of each packet. With the first card, you say, "Four." With the next, you say, "Five." Continue until you deal the card numbered 11.

"Jenny, let's see if these cards in any way match." Turn them over and hold them side by side. "Perfect! How symbolic! You chose two beautiful ladies."

Notes

(1) If you do the trick for a man, you might prefer to use kings or jacks. At the end, you comment, "You chose two handsome men."

(2) When dealing the cards simultaneously, you might find it easier to pick the cards off from the rear, fingers on top, and thumb below.

What a Coincidence!

I believe it was the legendary mentalist Ted Annemann who came up with this psychological force.

The problem is this: Occasionally, the force doesn't work. What do you do? You might indicate that since mentalism isn't an exact science, you can't always be perfect. Or you might explain that the vibrations weren't just right. Still, it would be nice to have some sort of satisfactory solution when you miss. I have a method here that works quite well.

The critical cards are these: king of hearts, seven of clubs, ace of diamonds, four of hearts, and the nine of diamonds. They are laid out in a row so that the spectator sees them in this order, the king of hearts being on his left.

You can remove these five cards from the deck one at a time and then lay them out in the proper order. Or you may prefer to have them sitting on top of the deck, ready for you to casually deal them into a face-up row.

The cards are laid out. Say to Bernie, "I wonder if you'd help me out. We have five cards here, and I'd like you to think of one.

"But before you do, I want you to look them over carefully so that your choice will be completely free. For instance, you might choose the king of hearts. Or maybe you think a face card is too obvious.

"Or you could choose the seven of clubs—a lucky card. But then it's the only black card.

"You could take the ace of diamonds, but maybe an ace is also too obvious. I don't know.

"The four of hearts? Some people associate hearts with romance, but others are reminded of a serious operation. It all depends.

"The nine of diamonds? Diamonds are forever. Maybe that's a good choice; maybe not.

"I'll look away while you think of one."

After he has one, turn back and pick up the five cards. Give them a little overhand shuffle. "Please concentrate on your card, Bernie."

Fan through the cards, faces towards yourself, as though studying them. From time to time, remove a card. Shake your head and replace it in the fan.

Continue moving cards around. Actually, you're setting them up so that from top to bottom (if the packet were face down) the order is four, seven, nine, king, ace—in other words, from lowest to highest.

"Bernie, we have to establish contact between you, the cards, and me." Set the packet of five onto the table. "Please give the cards a cut." He does so. Perhaps have him do it again.

"Good!" Pick up the packet, glance at the faces, and cut the cards so that the seven becomes the bottom card (the card at the face of the packet). The order of the cards is now nine, king, ace, four, seven. You're holding the cards in a fan, faces toward yourself.

"Bernie, you're thinking of your card, right? Now I'll give you a card which will indicate your thought."

Remove the four of hearts and place it face down onto his extended palm. "Please place your other hand on top of it. Good. Now you're holding the card and there's no way in the world I can change it." Pause. "Name your card."

He names the four of hearts. "Please show everyone the card you're holding."

That's what happens most of the time. But Bernie might choose another card, just to annoy you.

You have alternatives. These are not necessarily wonderful, but they do provide an adequate conclusion in the rare instances when the four is not chosen.

The packet is set up so that you can spell out any of the other four cards. The remaining possibilities are seven, nine, king, ace—again, lowest to highest. You'll spell F–O–U–R for the seven and nine; you'll spell F–O–U–R and then H–E–A–R–T–S for the king and ace.

So, if Bernie names the seven or nine, you say, "Turn over the card, please." He does. "As I said, the four should indicate your thought."

If Bernie names the king or ace, tell him to turn over the card.

Continue: "As I said, the four of hearts should indicate your thought." In either instance, add: "Let's see if it works."

Let's say Bernie has said that his card is the seven of clubs.

"We'll spell out 'four.' "

Say the letter F, moving one card from the top to the bottom of the packet. Do the same for the letters O and U. When you say the letter R, however, turn over the top card. It's the seven.

If Bernie says that his card is the nine (next highest), spell out F–O–U–R, moving one card from top to bottom for each letter. Turn up the card now on top. It's the nine.

The next highest card is the king. You have told Bernie that the four of hearts should indicate his thought. Continue: "First, we have the 'four.' "

Spell out F–O–U–R, moving one card from top to bottom for each letter.

"Then 'hearts.' "

Spell H–E–A–R–T–S, moving one card from top to bottom for each letter except the S. When you say the letter S, turn over the top card, showing the king.

For the ace, spell out F–O–U–R, exactly as you did for the king. Then spell H–E–A–R–T–S, moving one card from top to bottom for each letter. Turn over the card that is now on top. It's the ace.

The First Quadruple Coincidence

A few years ago I invented a trick that I called "Quadruple Coincidence." Soon after, I came across an older trick of the same name, invented, I believe, by Frank Garcia. Offhand, I can't think of a better impromptu trick. It dawned on me a short while ago that a basic component of the trick is a discovery of mine from many, many years ago.

Phil doesn't believe in mentalism in any form, so he's the perfect assistant. Hand him the deck of cards and ask him to shuffle.

Take the deck back and hold it up so that the back of the deck is toward the spectators.

"I need a prediction card," you declare. Note the value of the bottom card.

Hold the deck face up so that all can see the cards. With your right hand, take the bottom card. Take the next card *on top of this.* Continue dealing cards, one on top of the other, until you've taken as many cards as you need to *spell out* the value of the bottom card.

For instance, suppose the bottom card is a three. As you take the cards, one on top of the other, into your right hand, spell to yourself, "T–H–R–E–E," taking one card for each letter. Place these five cards face down on the table to your right. So, on the table is a pile of five cards, the top card of which is the one you saw on the bottom of the deck, a three.

"Don't worry, I'll find a good prediction card." Again, start taking cards one on top of the other into your right hand until you come to a card which matches the original bottom card—in this instance, another three. The three, then, is the last card you take into your right hand. Turn the cards in your right hand face down and place the group on top of the pile on the table. In our example, you now have two threes together, fifth and sixth from the bottom of the face-down pile on the table.

"Need a prediction," you mumble. At this point, if you wish, you can stop taking the cards one on top of the other; instead, just fan rapidly through the cards until you come to another three. This three you cut to the *back* of the face-up cards you're holding. (In other words, the three would be the top card if the packet were face down.)

At this point, tilt the deck toward you so that spectators can't see the faces of the cards. Fan through to the fourth three. Without letting the group see its face, place this three face down well in front of you.

"At last, my prediction!"

Place the rest of the cards in your hand face down onto the pile on the table. In our example, a face-down three is set forward as your prediction card, the top card of the deck is a three, and the fifth and sixth cards from the bottom are threes.

Pick up the deck and turn it face up. Rapidly deal the cards into a face-up pile. After you've dealt 15 or so, say to Phil, "You can tell me to stop anytime.

When you're told to stop, pick up the pile you've dealt off, turn it face down, and set it down to your right. Place the packet remaining in your left hand face down to your left.

"You chose when to stop, Phil. Now please touch one of the piles. We'll use the one you choose."

Suppose he chooses the pile on your left. "All right," you say. Turn over the top card of the pile and replace it, face up, onto the pile. "So you chose a three. Let's spell that out." Pick up the other pile. Spell T–H–R–E–E aloud, dealing one card into a pile for each letter in the spelling.

If Phil should touch the pile on your right, say, "All right, we'll spell down in the pile you've chosen." As before, you turn over the top card of the pile on the left and spell out that value in the pile on your right.

In either instance, you touch the last card dealt out and say, "Wouldn't it be a coincidence if this turned out to be a three also?" Turn the card over, showing that it is a three, and place it face up on top of the others you dealt off. Place the remainder of the deck directly in front of you.

The cards on the table should now form a diamond pattern, as in Illus. 25.

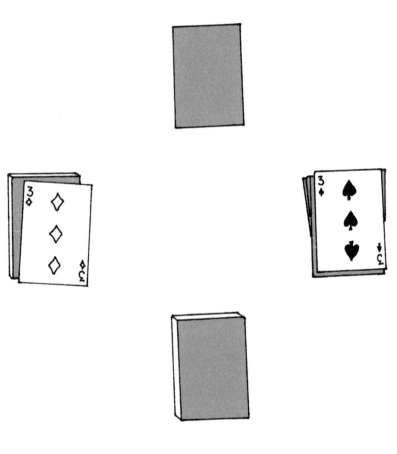

Illus. 25

"Wouldn't it be even more of a coincidence if my prediction card turned out to be a similar card?"

Turn over your prediction, showing it to be a three.

Touch the pile directly in front of you. "And what must this card be?" Turn it over to show that it also is a three.

Review

(1) A spectator shuffles the deck. You take it back, saying, "I need a prediction card."

(2) Hold the deck face up and note the value of the bottom card. Let's assume that it's a three. Silently spell out the value of this card, taking one card under the other for each letter. In this instance, spell out T–H–R–E–E. Place this pile face down onto the table.

(3) Continue going through the deck, taking one card on top of the other, until you come to another three, which will be the last card you take into your right hand. Place this pile face down on top of the first pile.

(4) Fan rapidly through the cards until you come to a third three. Cut the cards so that this three becomes the top card.

(5) Tilt the deck toward you so that others can't see the cards. Fan through to the fourth three. Without letting anyone else see its face, place it face down well forward of you. "At last, my prediction!"

(6) Place the rest of the cards in your hand face down on top of the pile on the table. Pick up the deck and turn it face up. Rapidly deal the cards into a face–up pile. After dealing 15 or so, ask a spectator to tell you when to stop.

(7) When stopped, turn the dealt-off cards face down. Place the remaining cards in your hand face down to the left of this pile.

(8) Ask a spectator to choose one of the piles. If he takes the one on your left, you turn over the top card of that pile and say, "So you chose a three. Let's spell that out." Pick up the other pile and spell T–H–R–E–E, dealing out one card for each letter in the spelling.

(9) If the spectator chooses the pile on your right, say, "We'll spell down in the pile you've chosen." As before, turn over the top card of the pile on your left and spell out the value in the other pile.

(10) Indicate that you're hoping for a coincidence as you turn over the last card you dealt out in the spelling. It is also a three. Turn it face up and place it on top of the cards you just dealt out.

(11) Place the remainder of the deck directly in front of you. The cards should now form a diamond pattern.

(12) Turn over your prediction card, showing that it's also a three.

(13) Turn over the top card of the remainder of the deck; it's the fourth three.

Notes

(1) Once in a while, this happens at the beginning of the trick: You note the bottom card and start to spell out its value, taking cards into your right hand. But one of these cards is of the same value as the bottom card. Obviously, the trick won't work. Give the deck a quick shuffle and start again.

(2) The placing of the four cards in a diamond formation is not only visually pleasing, but also provides a dramatic touch which enhances the trick considerably. It makes sense, therefore, to pause after the revelation of the fourth card, letting all enjoy the configuration and the startling climax.

Is My Face Red?

A familiar theme in card magic is this: Spectators try to guess whether face-down cards are red or black, with perfect success. In this version, I have superimposed some humor and excellent spectator participation. Furthermore, I have developed a way of secretly setting up the deck while spectators watch.

Solicit the aid of Cathie and Dobie. Have them each give the deck a shuffle.

Take the cards back, saying, "Cathie and Dobie, I'd like you to participate in a little contest. We'll see which one of you is better at identifying colors."

Fan the cards out, faces toward you. Pick out a card and hold it up, its back toward Cathie.

"Is this card red, Cathie? Yes or no." Whatever she answers, show the face of the card. Comment on her decision. Set the card aside face down.

Show Dobie the back of a card. Ask him, "Is this card black, Dobie? Yes or no." He answers; you show him the face of the card, make a comment, and set the card aside, on top of Cathie's first choice.

Again show Cathie the back of a card, asking her if it's red. Go through the same procedure as before. Repeat the process with Dobie, asking him if his card is black.

You continue, asking Cathie if she thinks the card is red and then asking Dobie if he thinks his card is black. Sometimes the card you hold up for Cathie is red, and sometimes it's black. And the same for Dobie. Each time that you set a card aside, you add it to a face-down pile.

Just keep going. For how long? For however long it takes you to get your cards set up.

When you first fan out the cards, you'll notice that, near the bottom, a number of red and black cards alternate. If this is not the case, cut the cards so that you do have a concentration of alternating reds and blacks near the bottom. You may find such a group with a few odd cards breaking up the perfect sequence. You will pick out these cards for Cathie and Dobie to guess.

Let's suppose that after Cathie and Dobie have made a few guesses, you have eight cards on the bottom alternating in color. Lift these off and place them onto the table in a face-down pile.

Give the remainder of the deck a little overhand shuffle. Turn the deck faces toward you again. Continue playing the game with Cathie and Dobie while actually you set up another bottom section to alternate reds and blacks. Again, if there is a preponderance of one color, you might have to cut the cards or even give them another shuffle. And feel free to shift a card or two as you try to decide which card to hold up next.

After Cathie and Dobie make additional guesses, you might have six, eight, or ten cards in appropriate alternating order. Place these face down on top of the pile you already have on the table.

You continue the process until you have at least 20 cards in the pile on the table.

Two things you must attend to:

(1) Always place an even number of cards onto the table.

(2) Remember the color of the original bottom card.

Following these two rules, you'll never get confused; you'll always end up with an even number of cards, and the cards will always alternate perfectly.

Let's suppose that the bottom card of the first pile is black. You must make sure that any other pile you place on top of it also has a black card on the bottom. And, since all piles are of an even number, the eventual top card will always be red.

This guessing procedure with Cathie and Dobie doesn't actually take very long. After each has made no more than five or six guesses, you should have your pile set up.

Meanwhile, you've been commenting on the choices made. Perhaps one contestant has been doing better than the other. In all probability, both have missed at least a few.

"That was the warm-up," you say. "Now we'll play for real. But I want each of you to do as well as you possibly can, so I'm going to place you both under a hypnotic spell." Wave your hands hypnotically before Cathie and Dobie. "You are weary, very weary. You are tired . . . tired. Bored, even. Now you're both under my spell. Will the miracles never stop?"

While gabbing away, set the balance of the deck on top of the pile of cards that Cathie and Dobie have guessed. Even up your pile of alternating reds and blacks. "Now you each must give this pile a cut." Make sure each gives the pile one *complete* cut. After they finish, pick up the cards and briefly tap them on the table on their long sides to even them up. The faces of the cards are toward you.

Actually, you're taking a peek at the bottom card to see what color it is.

If the bottom card is black, then the top card must be red; and vice versa. So let's say that when you peek at the bottom card, you see that it's black. Since Cathie has always been asked if she thinks the card is *red*, she must begin.

Set the packet between the two contestants.

Say to Cathie, "Do you think the top card is red, Cathie?"

If she says yes, continue, "Then just take that top card and, without looking at it, put it face down in front of you."

If she says no, say, "Then just take that top card and, without looking at it, place it on top of the rest of the deck." Indicate the pile where you put the previously guessed cards and the balance of the deck.

Ask Dobie if he thinks the next top card is black. If he thinks so, he places the card face down in front of him. Otherwise, he places it on top of the remainder of the deck.

"Your turn, Cathie. Is it red?" She makes her decision,

Dobie then decides if the next card is black.

They continue until the pile is exhausted. You, of course, interject comments, like, "Well, you have to take *some* cards," or, "They can't *all* be black."

Pick up the discards and casually give them a little shuffle as you proceed. "Let's see who the winner is. Turn your cards over, Cathie." She does. When she spreads them out, everyone sees that they're all red.

"And now you, Dobie." He has all black cards.

"A tie!" you declare. "You both got them all right."

Pause.

"I'd like to congratulate you, but my hypnotic spell did the job. I'm going to keep you under that spell so that you'll both be absolutely *right*–for the rest of your lives."

A Psychic Test

In its effect, this trick is somewhat similar to the preceding one. The basic secret is well known among magicians. I have made several changes in both presentation and method to eliminate sleight of hand and to make the trick impromptu.

Start by asking Lorne if he has any psychic powers. Whatever he replies, say, "I know that you have strong psychic powers, Lorne. In fact, I feel that you're sending me a mental message that you'd like me to test those powers of yours. Would you like to do that?"

He accepts the invitation.

You take a deck of cards, saying, "We'll need 13 pairs for this test," you say, "each pair a red and a black. I know that 13 is bad luck, but I think it might turn out to be a good-luck number for you."

Fan through the cards face up so that all can see. Remove from the deck a pair of cards—one black, one red. The black card should be uppermost. As you remove the pair, say to yourself, "Black and red." Make sure everyone sees the pair (Illus. 26).

Illus. 26

Turn the pair face down and set it on the table, saying, "One pair." Pause. "Would you all keep count with me. We must have exactly 13 pairs."

Take out another mixed pair, this time with the red card uppermost. As you do so, say to yourself, "Red and black." Display the pair, and then place it face down on top of the first pair, saying, "Two pairs."

Continue alternating black-and-red pairs with red-and-black pairs until you have 13 pairs in a face-down pile. You now have a red card on top, followed by a pair of blacks, a pair of reds, a pair of blacks, and so forth. The bottom card is black, and you have a pair of reds above it.

Set aside the rest of the deck. Even up the pile and have the packet cut three times, because "three is a lucky number." After three cuts, the deck is still set up in a continuous series of pairs which match in color. (There could be a single black card or a single red card on the bottom; if so, it will match in color the card on top.) Two cards, however, break up this series; they are the original top and bottom cards of the packet. Thumb through the packet, faces toward yourself, until you find these two cards (Illus. 27).

The two of spades and the ace of hearts break up the pattern.

Illus. 27

In Illus. 27, on the previous page, you can see that the two of spades and the ace of hearts are the two that break up the series. Once they are removed, the series of red and black pairs will be perfect.

Here's how you remove them: Say, "We'll need a couple of markers." With the cards still facing you, cut the deck so that these two cards come to the top. In this instance, you cut the cards so that the two of spades comes to the top, while the second card from the top is the ace of hearts. Turn the packet face down.

Deal the top card face up onto the table, saying, "A black card." Deal the present top card face up onto the table next to the first card, saying, "And a red card." Turn the packet face down and set it on the table. You now have a pair of black cards on top, followed by alternating pairs of red and black.

"Lorne, we have 12 pairs left. If you get six of these right, that would be about average. But I *know* that you have psychic powers, so my guess is that you'll get at least seven or eight of these right."

Lift off the top two cards from the packet on the table. Mix them a bit as you say, "Which one of these cards do you think is black?"

Since both cards are black, his chances of getting it right are excellent. Whichever he chooses, place it face down on the black marker. Place the other card on top of the remainder of the deck.

Treat the next pair the same way, asking him to choose which card he thinks is red. Continue through the rest of the pairs, alternating the colors. At the end, you show that he did not get seven or eight right—he got them *all* right.

"Good heavens, Lorne! You're far more psychic than I thought you were."

Note

If you start by asking the spectator which card he thinks is the *red* one, and continue alternating colors, he will miss every one.

This can be amusing, proving that he has no psychic ability whatever (or has *inverse* psychic ability). But I prefer the other version, which is more upbeat and leaves everyone happy.

They Always Get Their Man

This is my slight variation of a trick by Phil Goldstein. I changed the working a bit and the patter quite a bit.

Fan through the deck and toss the red jacks face up onto the table.

Explain to the group, "You've probably heard stories of the valiant Canadian Mounted Police, or, as they are sometimes known, the Mounties. Who can tell me what they're best known for?"

Someone is bound to get the right answer: "They always get their man."

"That's right. And we're going to put that theory to the test. We'll see if the sterling qualities of the Mounties can be transferred to the playing cards which represent them."

Point to the face-up red jacks on the table.

"Here we have two Mounties. I'm sure you notice their traditional red jackets."

Rosemarie has always had an interest in officers of the law, so ask her to assist you.

Casually fan seven cards from the top of the deck. Lift them off and hand them to Rosemarie, saying, "Rosemarie, I'd like you to pick a criminal from those cards. You can either choose one from the underworld . . ." Indicate the bottom card of the packet: ". . . or you can choose one from the top echelons of crime."

Indicate the top card.

"So, when you're done shuffling, look at either the top or bottom card. But don't do it just yet. After you've chosen a criminal, you'll perform a peculiar shuffle. Then I'll put one of the Mounties on top of the packet and one on the bottom, and you'll perform the same kind of shuffle again. But you don't have to remember all of that. We'll take it step by step. So, when you're ready, look at the top or bottom card."

If she looks at the *top* card, she performs an *under-down* shuffle: She places the top card on the bottom of the packet, the next card onto the table, the next card on the bottom, the next card on top of the one on the table, etc. When she is left with one card in her hand, she places this on top of those on the table.

You lead her through the shuffle, saying, "Put the top card on the bottom of the packet, deal the next card onto the table, put the next one on the bottom of the packet . . ."

If she looks at the *bottom* card, she performs a *down-under* shuffle. The first card goes onto the table, the next one on the bottom of the packet, the next onto the table, etc. And, as before, the last card she holds goes onto the pile on the table. Again, lead her through the shuffle.

"So now our criminal is buried somewhere in the packet. These two jacks are supposed to be Mounties, so let's see if they can behave like Mounties. The packet you're holding, Rosemarie, represents a big mountain with thousands of trees on it. The Mounties know that the criminal is somewhere on the mountain, so they're going to search it from top to bottom."

Hand her one of the red jacks face up. "Please put one Mountie on top of the packet face up." Hand her the other jack. "And put the other Mountie on the bottom of the packet face up."

When she finishes, hold out your left hand palm up. "Please place the packet onto my hand."

After she does, place your right hand on top and give the cards a quick shake. "This gets them started on their search." Lift up your right hand and have her take the packet back.

"Now, Rosemarie, you must take them on their search."

This time, she will *always* perform an under-down shuffle. "Put the top card on the bottom, deal the next card onto the table, put the next card on the bottom, deal the next card on top of the card on the table."

If necessary, take her through it the rest of the way. In all likelihood, however, she won't need any coaching after the first two cards.

Take the cards from the table. Fan them out. Fan down to the face-up red jacks. Between them is a face-down card. Remove all three together and set them onto the table. *Put the rest of the cards on top of the deck.*

"Well, the Mounties captured someone. Let's see how they did. Rosemarie, what's the name of the criminal you chose?"

After she names the card, you turn over the "captured" card.

"So the Mounties got their man. But how did those jacks *know* they were Mounties?

"And how did they find their man? Who knows? You know what I think? I think it's just coincidence."

At this point, you'll probably get some sarcastic comments from the group.

Notes

(1) Putting the remainder of the packet back on top at the end of the trick is important. A spectator trying to reconstruct the trick will find it extremely difficult without knowing the correct number of cards. In fact, after the trick is over, a spectator will sometimes ask, "How many cards did you give me?" As usual, I lie, saying, "I don't know. I didn't notice." This clearly implies that the number is irrelevant.

(2) Early on, you tell your assistant that she'll perform a peculiar shuffle and that later, she'll perform the same kind of shuffle. But even when she performs a down-under shuffle the first time, she *must* perform an under-down shuffle the second time. Does this make you an obvious liar? Not really. The shuffles are the "same kind"; they're just not identical. So far, no one has called me on there being a difference between the two. If anyone ever says to me, "Hey, those two shuffles are different," I'll reply, "Of course," and continue on.

A Subtle Touch

As far as I know, the method involved here is my invention. The main feature of the trick is that you never touch the cards.

Hand Francine the deck and ask her to mix the cards. When she finishes and tries to return the deck to you, comment, "No, no. I want the deck to remain in your hands throughout the experiment."

Pause to make sure this selling-point sinks in. "Now I'd like you to deal the cards into a face-up pile. Deal as many as you want. I'll turn my back, so when you're done, be sure to tell me. Otherwise, this could be an extremely long experiment. Go ahead, you can start dealing."

As Francine begins dealing, you count the first several cards mentally to get the pace. Then you turn away, but continue to count at the same pace. When Francine says she's done, stop counting. But be sure to remember the number you counted to—your *key number*.

With your back still turned to the group, give Francine these directions: "Look at the last card you dealt and remember it. That's your chosen card. Now pick up the pile you dealt off, turn it face down, and put it back on top of the deck."

When Francine is done, you turn and face the group once more. Now you have a bit of simple math to do. You subtract eight from your key number. Let's suppose your key number is 14. You subtract eight, giving you six.

"Francine, I need to find my lucky card. Please slowly deal the cards into a face-up pile. When you get to my lucky card, I'll stop you."

Actually, you're not looking for a lucky card; you want to stop her after she has dealt out the sixth card. Why the sixth card? Because six is the result of subtracting eight from your key number, 14.

If you had counted to 19 originally, then 19 would be your key number. You'd subtract eight from 19, getting 11. In this instance, you'd stop Francine after she had dealt 11 cards.

Back to our original example: Francine has dealt out six cards face up and you've stopped her. But you don't simply stop her; after all, you want to conceal the fact that you've been counting.

So here's what you do: Suppose the sixth card she deals is the nine of clubs; you say, "That's it! The nine of clubs—my lucky card!" Naturally, she stops dealing.

"I'm going to need my lucky card, so would you please hand it to me. It's curious, but nearly every time I hold my lucky card, a peculiar coincidence occurs. Let's see if it happens again." She gives you the card. Point to the remaining cards that she just dealt out. "Turn these face down on the table."

She does. "Please put the rest of the deck on top of the pile."

After she's done, say, "For this to work, Francine, you'll have to deal out five cards in a row. So far, you've done all the dealing face up, so you might as well continue doing that."

She does so. Continue, with appropriate pauses: "Now deal another card face up on top of each one. Continue until you have seven face-up cards in each pile. As we all know, seven is one of the most powerful numbers in magic."

After Francine has finished dealing, her chosen card should be second from the bottom (or sixth from the face) in one of the five face-up piles.

"I feel strongly that your card is in one of the piles, Francine."

Hold your lucky card up to your ear and listen intently for a moment.

"In fact, my lucky card is sure of it. Are we right?"

You are. "Good. Please pick up that pile."

Francine is holding the pile face up. "Just a second," you say.

Hold your lucky card up to your ear again and listen for a moment.

"My lucky card says that you should do a down-under shuffle. If all goes well, you'll end up with your chosen card. Just deal that first card onto the table. Then put the next card on the bottom of your pile. The next card goes on the table, and the next one goes to the bottom of the pile."

Francine continues until she's holding one face-up card.

"Don't keep us in suspense, Francine. Is that your card?"

It is.

The only time the trick fails is when Francine changes her pace when originally dealing out the cards. Even then, the trick might work, because you can be off as many as two cards on either side of the correct number and still be successful.

So, unlikely as the possibility is, suppose the trick just didn't work. What do you do? I don't know. The one time that it happened to me, I blamed my lucky card and declared vehemently that I was dumping it and getting myself a new lucky card.

TELEPATHY OR THOUGHT TRANSFERENCE

The Acting Magician

Are you a good actor? If not, here you have a chance to sharpen up your acting skills.

If you *are* a good actor, this trick is perfect for you. I developed this trick to take advantage of my own ability to appear utterly serious as I present the most inane propositions. The principle used here is quite venerable.

At the beginning, you must know the names of the top and bottom cards. Rather than strain my memory, I usually place the ace of spades on top of the deck and the ace of clubs on the bottom. Let's assume that you do the same.

Take the deck from the card case and give the cards a riffle shuffle, keeping the ace of spades on top and the ace of clubs on the bottom. This is quite easy to do, as you'll see when you give it a try.

Set the deck on the table. If you hand it to a spectator at this point, he just might idly shuffle the cards, which would ruin the trick.

Ambrose is good at following instructions, so enlist his aid.

Say, "Ambrose, I'd like you to think of any number from one to ten. Do you have a number? Good. Now, please change your mind and choose another number. I want to make sure everyone knows that this is not a psychological stunt."

Once Ambrose has his number, continue: "Now please think of a suit—clubs, hearts, spades, or diamonds. Put that together in your mind and you are thinking of a specific playing card. By the way, if you thought of the number one, that would be an ace, of course. Next, with your help, I'll try to divine the name of that card."

Turn your back and say, "Concentrate on the value of your card, please." After a moment, say, "I can't seem to get it. Maybe we can make the thought waves more concrete. Would you pick up the deck and deal into a pile a number of cards equal to the value of the card you thought of. For instance, if you thought of the number eight, please deal eight cards into a pile. But deal very quietly so that I won't hear how many you're dealing."

Chat for a moment of the difficulties you're encountering. Then continue: "I'm still not getting it, Ambrose. Let's try something else; we'll get back to the value. Concentrate on the color of the card you chose, Ambrose. Think red . . . or black." Pause. "It's not clear. Do me a favor. If the card is red, very quietly deal one card onto your pile. If not, don't deal anything."

A brief pause.

"I'm not getting it. Back to the value. Ambrose, again would you deal a number equal to the value of your card onto your pile."

Once more, you complain bitterly of the tremendous task you've undertaken. "Gosh! I just *can't* get the value. Let's try the suits again. Ambrose, if the card you're thinking of is a spade or diamond, please quietly deal *two* cards onto the pile. Otherwise, do nothing." Pause.

"I can't understand it. Nothing seems to work. Maybe if I actually see the faces of the cards, I can figure it out. Ambrose, place the rest of the cards you're holding on top of the cards you've dealt off. Even all the cards up."

At this point, you turn back to the group; you want to make sure that Ambrose gives the deck a proper cut when you provide the next instruction.

"Please give the deck a complete cut. And you can give the cards another cut if you wish." Since a complete cut doesn't destroy the basic order of the cards, he can cut them any number of times.

Take the deck from Ambrose and hold it so that you are looking at the face of the bottom card. Begin fanning through the cards. "Maybe if I *see* your card, I'll know it."

You are looking for the ace of spades, the first card Ambrose dealt off. When you get to the ace of spades, mentally count it as one. Continue counting the cards as you fan through the deck, until you get to the ace of clubs. Count the card *before* the ace of clubs, but do not count the ace of clubs. (While fanning through the deck, it is more efficient—and less obvious that you are counting—if you count by threes.) The number of cards you counted is the same number as Ambrose counted into his pile. This is your *key number.* You must remember this number; it not only will tell you the value of the chosen card, but also the suit.

Here's what you do to determine the value of the thought-of card: Divide the key number by two. (*Disregard the remainder.*) Either this will be the value of the card, or the card will be the next lower value. How can you tell which is correct? Easy. Just find out whether the chosen card is odd or even.

Suppose that the key number is 14. You divide this by two, getting seven. Since seven is an odd number, you say, "Ambrose, I get a strong feeling that your card is an odd-numbered card, is that right?" If he says yes, you know that the value actually is seven. If he says no, you know that the value is the next lower number, six.

Suppose that the key number is 21. You divide this by two, getting ten. (There is a remainder of one, but you *always disregard the remainder.*) Since ten is an even number, you say, "Ambrose, I get a strong feeling that your card is an even-numbered card, is that right?" If he says yes, you know that the value actually is ten. If he says no, you know that the value is the next lower number, nine.

Incidentally, when you get a positive answer to your query, say, "I thought so." When you get a negative answer, say, "So much for strong feelings. I'd better concentrate harder."

At this point in the performance, you should pause and mentally review your calculations to make sure you have the right value.

Once you have the value of the thought-of card, the rest is easy. For the suit, double the value of the chosen card and subtract that amount from the key number. (Say the value of the chosen card is six and the key number is 14. Double six, giving you 12. Subtract 12 from 14, getting two.) If the result is zero, the suit is clubs; if the result is one, the suit is hearts; if the result is two, the suit is spades; if the result is three, the suit is diamonds. This order is easily remembered by using this mnemonic:

CHaSeD—Clubs, Hearts, Spades, Diamonds

0 = Clubs, 1 = Hearts, 2 = Spades, 3 = Diamonds

Once you have figured out the suit and value, fan through the deck, remove the thought-of card, and place it face down onto the table. Ask Ambrose to name his card. Have him turn the tabled card face up.

Review

(1) You have the ace of spades on top of the deck and the ace of clubs on the bottom.

(2) Turn your back and have the spectator think of any number from one to ten. To this, he mentally adds a suit.

(3) He deals a number equal to the value of his card into a pile.

(4) Onto that same pile, he deals one card if his card is red and none if his card is black.

(5) He again deals a number equal to the value of his card onto the pile.

(6) He deals two cards onto the pile if his card is a spade or a diamond (the last two suits in the mnemonic CHaSeD).

(7) He places the rest of the deck on top of the pile. Then he gives the deck as many complete cuts as he wishes.

(8) Starting at the bottom of the deck, you fan through, looking at the faces of the cards. When you reach the ace of spades, you count it as one and continue counting until you reach the ace of clubs. You count the card before the ace of clubs, but not the ace itself. This is your key number.

(9) Divide the key number by two. (*Disregard the remainder.*) The thought-of card is either this number or the next lower number.

(10) If the result of dividing the key number by two is an odd number, say that you think the thought-of card is odd. If the spectator agrees, your number is correct; if he denies this, the selection is the next lower number. If the result of dividing the key number by two is an even number, say that you think the card is even. If the spectator agrees, your number is correct; if he denies it, the selection is the next lower number.

(11) Double the value of the chosen card and subtract that amount from the key number. The result tells you the suit:

$$0 = \textbf{Clubs}$$
$$1 = \textbf{Hearts}$$
$$2 = \textbf{Spades}$$
$$3 = \textbf{Diamonds}$$

An Old-Timer

Here's a trick so old that it has long since been forgotten by most older magicians and is unknown to younger ones. In its original form, it was colorful and effective. I have revitalized the trick, providing an improved handling and a new climax. Also, there is a one-in-five chance of performing a miracle.

Ask Paul to shuffle the deck. Take the cards back, saying, "I'm going to deal out some cards, forming a mystical pattern." You deal the cards face up like this:

		1		2		
	3	4	5	6	7	
		8		9		
	10	11	12	13	14	
		15		16		

"Paul, you'll notice that there are four rows of five cards each."

(Actually, there are two rows and two columns, but the spectators generally don't care about this distinction.) You indicate each of the rows by running your hand across or down it (Illus. 28).

"Please think of any one of these cards." Avert your head as he does so.

"Now, with my mysterious, mystical, magical powers, I'll identify the very card you thought of." Stare briefly into Paul's eyes. Study the cards carefully. Another stare into Paul's eyes. "But it might take me a little while. I'm just not getting it."

At last, an inspiration: "Paul, your card could be in one of four rows or it could be all by itself. Wherever it is, would you please pick up a row which contains your card." He picks up one of the rows. (He can pick up the cards in any order.)

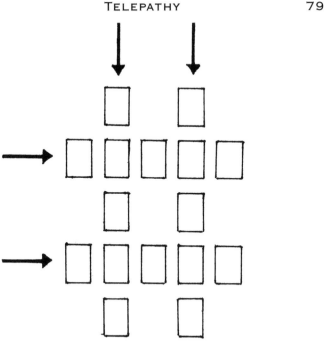

Illus. 28

After Paul has picked up his row, only one other five-card row remains. You pick that one up.

"Please mix up your cards, like this." Give the cards you picked up a quick overhand shuffle.

After Paul mixes his five cards, take them from him and place them face down on top of the face-down pile you're holding.

Pick up the remaining six cards that are on the table and put them face down on top of all.

"Here, I'll give them a little extra mixing." You now perform my *One–Two–Three Shift* (explained in detail starting on page 7). In this instance, you transfer 11 cards from the top of the pile to the bottom.

Drop the packet on top of the deck, saying, "Maybe we should try an even more mystical pattern."

Pick up the deck and deal 11 cards face up in this order:

```
1      2              3      4

              5

6      7              8      9

10                           11
```

You deal the next four cards so that each one lands in one of the positions marked with an X. It doesn't matter which one goes where.

```
X                            X

1      2      X      3      4

              5

6      7      X      8      9

10                           11
```

Any X could be the chosen card. Also, the top card of the deck could be the chosen card. "Notice that in this formation, there are four rows with five cards in each row." As before, indicate each row by running your hand along it. Two of the rows are diagonal and two are horizontal (Illus. 29).

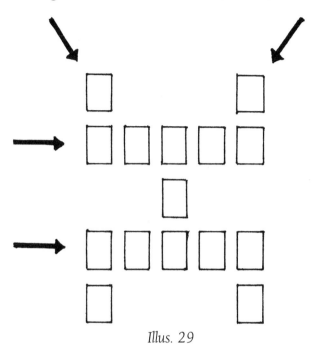

Illus. 29

Again, stare into Paul's eyes and then study the cards. "No good," you declare at length. "What row is your card in?" As soon as he indicates a row, you know the chosen card, for it's the only X card in that row. A good conclusion is to pass your hand over the row slowly, back and forth, finally letting it fall onto the chosen card. "Is this it?" you ask. Naturally.

Suppose, however, that you ask which row the card is in, and Paul looks puzzled, finally telling you that his card isn't there. "Of course not," you say. "It's right here." Flip the top card of the deck face up.

As you can see, this superior ending will occur, on the average, once every five times.

The Name Doesn't Matter

Arun Bonerjee came up with an excellent trick based on a principle that is fairly well known among magicians. Wally Wilson showed me his version, in which he added a few subtle touches. I also added a touch or two.

Since Ginger really pays attention, she is the perfect choice to be your assistant. Hand her the deck and ask her to give it a shuffle.

"Now please deal the cards into a pile on the table."

She might ask, "How many?" or, "All of them?"

You say, "It doesn't matter."

But, of course, it *does* matter, at least to you. As she deals the cards, you apparently pay no attention, but actually count them.

She may deal only a small number of cards. When this happens, say, "Go ahead. We should have a fairly substantial pile."

After Ginger has dealt 13 or so, say, "Stop whenever you wish."

In any instance, make sure you know the number she finally deals. Let's say the number is 17.

You turn your back.

"I'd like you to mentally picture a pair of dice. In your mind, please select one of those dice. Roll that die and look at the number on top. But don't choose that number. Roll that die again. Do you see the number on top?

"Good. That's your number." Clearly, you're asking her to choose a number from one to six, but this method enhances the trick and sets the tone for the superb mental climax.

"Ginger, please quietly count that number of cards from your packet and hide them somewhere. Put them in your pocket or under something so that I won't be able to see them.

"Now please take a look at the card that lies at that number from the top of your packet. Remember that card and leave it at that position in the packet. In other words, if you hid three cards, you'd look at the third card from the top of the packet."

When she's done, turn back to the group.

"Ginger, if this is going to work, we'll require the strength of at least two people—you and one other person. So would you please think of the first name of someone you admire. What is that name?"

She tells you. Let's suppose the name is Ralph. "Please spell out that name, moving one card from the top to the bottom of your pile for each letter."

If you haven't already figured out the number of letters in the name, count them to yourself as she moves the cards from the top to the bottom of the pile. In this instance, you count five cards for R–A–L–P–H.

You now have two numbers in mind: the number she dealt off originally—in this example, 17; and the number in the name she spelled—in this case, five.

Subtract the number of cards in the name (five) from the total she dealt off at the beginning (17). Seventeen minus five gives you 12. This is the number of cards you must move from the top to the bottom of the packet.

"I'll mix the cards a bit."

You now perform my *One–Two–Three Shift* (explained in detail starting on page 7), transferring 12 cards from the top to the bottom of the packet. This brings the chosen card to the bottom of the packet. (I know that this doesn't seem likely, but it nonetheless works.)

In some sneaky way, you must now peek at that bottom card. Here are three possibilities; choose whichever one seems most natural to you:

(1) After you mix the cards, briefly tap them onto the table on their long sides to even them up. The backs are toward the spectators, and the faces are toward you. Thus, you can easily catch a glimpse of the bottom card. Hand the packet to Ginger and ask her to give them an additional shuffle.

(2) Ask Ginger to give the cards a shuffle. Grip the packet at the rear end with your right hand, fingers on top and thumb on the bottom. As you hand the packet to Ginger, tip it forward

ever so slightly so that you can get a peek at the bottom card (Illus. 30).

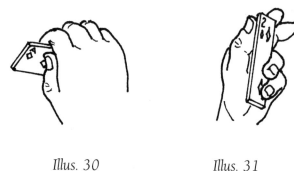

Illus. 30   Illus. 31

(3) Turn slightly to the right as you comment, "You know, Ginger, you really ought to shuffle the cards too." You're holding the cards in your left hand in the position preceding an over-hand shuffle. Let the cards tilt a bit toward the group (Illus. 31). Glance down, taking a quick look at the bottom card, as you take the cards in your right hand and perform a brief overhand shuffle. (It's perfectly natural that you should take a look at your hands as you begin the shuffle.) Immediately hand the packet to Ginger for her to mix the cards.

As Ginger shuffles the cards, provide this review: "I had no way of knowing what number you'd think of, nor could I know what name you'd come up with. So if I go through the packet and find your card, would that be a good trick?"

The correct answer is yes. "Well, I don't want to do a trick. Instead, I'd like to try to read your mind. Fan the cards out, faces toward you, please. Now place your finger on your chosen card and concentrate on it."

Pause. "And, wherever you are, Ralph, please help her concentrate." After a suitable pause, you gradually reveal the card—first, naming the color, then the suit, and finally the value.

Note

As you no doubt have discerned, the whole business of having her think of a name and spell it out is nothing more than a smoke screen.

A Kingly Decision

Joe Hustler invented this extraordinarily effective trick. You must perform it to see what a strong result you get with a minimum amount of labor. A modest amount of preparation is necessary.

Remove from the deck the four kings. Place the king of clubs on top. The other three kings should be placed near the bottom. I generally put one on the bottom, one third from the bottom, and one fifth from the bottom.

Darla is excellent at shuffling the cards, so you should solicit her help. But first, you have some shuffling of your own to do. Give the deck two good riffle shuffles.

Hand the deck to Darla, saying, "Please give the cards a little over-hand shuffle."

Once she takes the deck, pantomime the over-hand shuffling motion. She should give the deck *only one* over-hand shuffle. If she looks as though she might continue shuffling, place your hand on top of her hands and say, "I want you to listen carefully." This effectively stops her from giving the cards the extra shuffle that will spoil the trick.

Turn away from the group. "Darla, hold the deck so that the faces are toward you and no one else can see the faces of any of the cards. Now fan through and take out the first king that you come to. Hide that card somewhere. You can put it into a pocket, sit on it, whatever."

The first king that she comes to is the king of clubs.

"Next, take out the king that's the same color as the one you took. Please put that king in Herb's pocket." Obviously, you name one of the males who is present.

Turn back and face the group. Concentrate fiercely. At length point at Herb and declare, "The card in your pocket, Herb, is the king of spades. And, of course, Darla's king is the king of clubs."

Triple Telepathy

Stewart Judah came up with the original trick. It is little known and its climax is absolutely astounding. I have changed the handling slightly.

A modest amount of memory work is required. You must remember the number of cards that a spectator deals, and, later, you must also remember the name of a specific card. Not too tough, actually.

Let's assume that three ladies agree to cooperate in an experiment in telepathy. We'll call them Spectators 1, 2, and 3.

Ask Spectator 1 to shuffle the deck. Take it back and silently count off 15 cards from the top. Count the cards by three so that it will not be obvious that you're counting them.

Hand the 15 cards to Spectator 1, saying, "Please shuffle these. Then deal as many of them as you wish into a pile. Look at the *last* card you deal into the pile and remember it. Put it back and place the rest of your cards on top of it."

Make sure your directions are understood.

The next few seconds are extremely critical. You must seem totally uninterested in what Spectator 1 is doing. Actually, you're counting the number of cards that she deals into a pile. *Remember* that number. Say it over to yourself several times till the end of the trick.

To cover the fact that you're counting the number of cards being dealt, you might act slightly befuddled, saying something like, "Let's see. Now who was our next volunteer?"

Point to the pile on the table, and address Spectator 2: "So far, we have one chosen card in the middle of a shuffled pile. Now, I'd appreciate it if you'd cut off a pile from the deck."

Hold out the remaining cards. After she cuts off a pile, continue, "Shuffle those and look at your bottom card. That will be your chosen card." As you say, "Shuffle those . . . ," do so with the cards you're holding. When you add, ". . . look at your bottom card," slightly tip the cards you're holding and take a casual glance at the bottom card. Remember this card; it's your *key card.* As Spectator 2 continues following your directions, give your packet another over-hand shuffle. Make sure you shuffle off the last few cards individually so that the bottom card, which you know, becomes the top card.

You are now remembering the number of cards that Spectator 1 dealt into a pile and the name of the top card of the packet you're holding—your key card.

Ask Spectator 2 to place her packet onto the table.

Approach Spectator 3, fanning the cards from hand to hand.

"Please take any one of these cards." After she selects a card, close up the cards and place them in a face-down pile onto the table. "Please look at your card and then place it on top of the pile." Point to the pile you just set onto the table.

Time to toss a bit of stardust into the eyes of all.

Point to the first pile, saying, "Now we have a card in the middle . . ." Point to the second pile. ". . . and a card on the bottom . . ." Point to the third pile. ". . . and a card on top. And all the piles have been shuffled. So let's lose that last card by placing *this* pile on top of it." Indicate that Spectator 1 should place her pile on top of Spectator 3's pile. Turn to Spectator 2. "And let's lose your card by placing your pile on top of all." Indicate that Spectator 2 should place her pile on top of the combined piles. Each spectator gives the deck one complete cut. "The deck is thoroughly mixed. Since there's no way I could know any one of the selected cards, I must try telepathy."

Ask Spectator 3 to concentrate. Fan through the cards, faces toward yourself, studying them carefully. Cut the key card to the top (or back) of the deck. The card that is facing you belongs to Spectator 3. Tentatively take it and place it face down in front of Spectator 3.

Turn to Spectator 1. "Please concentrate on your card also." Now you must recall the number that Spectator 1 dealt off at the beginning. Starting with the card that is now on the bottom, count that many. The card at that number from the bottom is Spectator 1's card. Ponder a bit, finally placing the card face down in front of Spectator 1.

Now it's Spectator 2's turn to concentrate. Continue counting from the previous number until you reach 15. *The next card* will be Spectator 2's. Place it face down in front of her.

Each spectator in turn names her card and turns it over.

Review

(1) Spectator 1 shuffles the deck and gives it back. You subtly count off 15 cards from the top of the deck and hand these to her, telling her to shuffle them, deal some into a pile, and then look at and remember the last card she deals. She replaces this card on the dealt-off pile and puts the remainder of the 15 cards on top.

(2) You seem to be paying no attention, but you actually count the number Spectator 1 deals off. You must remember that number.

(3) Hold out the remainder of the deck to Spectator 2, asking her to cut off a pile. She shuffles these and then looks at and remembers the bottom card.

(4) As you demonstrate how Spectator 2 is to shuffle her cards, you sneak a peek at the bottom card of those remaining in your hand. With an over-hand shuffle, you move this card to the top of the packet. You are now remembering two things: the number of cards counted off by Spectator 1 and the name of the card on top of the packet you're holding—your key card.

(5) Tell Spectator 2 to place her packet onto the table.

(6) Fan the cards you're holding from hand to hand, asking Spectator 3 to choose one. After she does, you close up the packet and place it face down onto the table. Spectator 3 looks at her card and then places it on top of the packet you just set onto the table.

(7) Have Spectator 1 put her pile on top of Spectator 3's pile. Have Spectator 2 put her pile on top of all.

(8) Each spectator gives the deck one complete cut.

(9) Fan through the cards, faces toward yourself. Cut the key card to the top (or back) of the deck. The card facing you is Spectator 3's. Place it face down in front of her.

(10) Recall the number that Spectator 1 dealt off. Starting with the card that is now at the face of the deck, count that many. The card at that number from the face of the deck is Spectator 1's. Place it face down in front of her.

(11) Continue counting from the previous number until you reach 15. The next card is Spectator 2's. Place it face down in front of her.

(12) Each spectator in turn names her card and then turns it over.

Behind the Back

Ronald J. Dayton came up with this very subtle idea: You look over the group carefully and then choose as your assistant Ralph, whom you know to be a good sport.

"Ralph, we're going to test your telepathic ability. Please turn away from the group for a moment."

While Ralph's back is turned, fan the deck out face up and have Gloria touch one of the cards. Close up the deck and tell Ralph that he can rejoin the group. In fact, you maneuver Ralph so that he's at the front of the group. You and he are facing everyone else.

"Ralph, I'm going to have you look right at the person who selected a card. As you do so, concentrate and see if the name of the card comes to you.

"The entire card may come to you in a flash. Or the card could come to you as a number and the initial of the suit. The six of clubs, for instance, could come to you as 6C." Maneuver Ralph so he's directly facing Gloria.

"Are you getting the name of the card, Ralph?" He is. What's more, he names the selected card.

You can repeat the stunt a time or two. Ralph might not get each selection perfectly, but he demonstrates absolutely that he has telepathic powers.

Is Ralph a confederate? Not to begin with. In fact, you could choose anyone who's a good sport.

As you maneuver Ralph around to face Gloria, you keep your right hand behind his back. After you explain how the card might come to him as a number and a digit, you *trace the name of the card on his back with your first finger.* If the selection were the eight of spades, you would trace *8S* on his back. If it were the queen of hearts, you would trace *QH.*

Ralph might not interpret your tracing perfectly, but he should get enough of it to demonstrate his amazing powers.

Note

For guaranteed results, you can work with someone you know and do some practice ahead of time.

No Sleight Trick

This trick originally called for considerable sleight of hand. I've eliminated this and added several possible conclusions.

Howard always seems quite suggestible, so he'd be perfect for this trick. Hand him the deck of cards and ask him to shuffle it.

"Now, Howard, please cut the deck into three fairly equal piles." Make sure the piles are nearly the same. If there is a disparity, you might say, "That's equal?"

When you're satisfied with the piles, say, "Howard, pick up any one of the piles, take a card from it, and show it around."

After he does so, say, "Set your pile back down onto the table and put your card on top of it." He does. "Even up your pile, cut it in the middle, and complete your cut." If Howard is as suggestible as you think, he should cut the pile quite close to the middle.

"Now set your pile on top of one of the others, and then place the last pile on top."

Howard's card is now quite close to the middle of the deck.

You take the deck and, cutting it as close as you can to the middle, riffle-shuffle the two halves together. As you take the two halves, preliminary to the shuffle you should be able to get a good look at the bottom card of one of the halves. Remember this card; it's your *key card*. And when you riffle-shuffle, make sure that this becomes the bottom card of the deck.

Invite Howard to give the deck a complete cut. Actually, the deck can be given any number of complete cuts. Spread the deck face up onto the table, fanning the cards out so that all can be seen.

"Howard, I'd like you to pick out five cards from various parts of the deck. And make one of them the card you chose. I'm going to watch closely, so be as sneaky as you can. It won't matter, really, because I'm certain I'll be able to read your mind."

As Howard starts to remove the cards, note where your key card is. His chosen card will either be the key card, or it will be very close to it. So if he takes one card from near the key card and four others from other spots in the deck, you're all set.

Take the five cards from Howard and place them in a face-up row on the table. Pass your hand over them until some mysterious force causes you to drop your hand on top of one card.

"I feel that this is your card, Howard."

All are dumbfounded.

They will probably be equally astounded if you use this conclusion: Howard is holding the five cards face up. You note at what position the chosen card lies. Ask him to turn the pile face down. If his chosen card is now second from the top, all is well. Otherwise, you must bring it to that position.

Suppose it's at the bottom of the pile. Say, "As you know, Howard, three is a mystic number. Please deal three cards into a pile. Now place the rest of your cards on top." His chosen card is now second from the top.

What if the chosen card is at the top of the pile? Have him deal off three cards, drop the rest on top, and then repeat the process. Again, the chosen card is second from the top.

If the chosen card is fourth from the top, have him turn his pile face up. The chosen card is now second from the top of the face-up pile.

If the chosen card is third, the procedure is slightly different, as I'll explain in a moment.

His chosen card is now second from the top of the group of five. You direct Howard through a down-under deal. "Please deal a card onto the table, and place the next card on the bottom of your packet. Deal another one onto the table, and put the next card on the bottom." He continues until he's holding only one card. It's the one he chose.

If Howard's card is third from the top, you have him perform an under-down deal. The first card goes under the packet, the next one goes onto the table, and so on. Again, he ends up with his selected card.

Note

When Howard picks out his five cards, he might just take two from fairly close to your key card. Clearly, the chosen card could be either one of these. When you take the five cards from him, arrange it so that these are the top two.

Study the faces of the cards. Note and remember the top card. "I can't seem to figure it out. I want these out of my sight while I concentrate." Stick the five cards into your pocket. After trancing for several seconds, remove four cards from your pocket, leaving the top one there.

Do not spread out the cards.

Hold the four cards in the dealing position in your left hand. Bring your right hand to the deck, ready to deal. "I believe I have your card, Howard. What is it?" There are two possibilities:

(1) If he does not name the card in your pocket, you know that it must be the top card of the packet. Deal it off the top of the packet, turning it over. "And there it is!" Return the rest of the packet to your pocket, adding the pocketed card to the bottom. "You know what the key is, don't you?" Pat your pocket. "Getting the cards out of sight." Bring out the four cards and add them to the deck. Put the chosen card face down on top of the deck as well.

(2) If Howard names the card in your pocket, immediately turn over the top card of the packet, saying, "That's not it." Drop the card face up onto the table. Continue in the same way with the other three cards. "I believe I have it . . ." Pull the chosen card from your pocket and show it. ". . . right here!"

The Force Is with You

The brilliant Wally Wilson recently developed a wonderful force which works particularly well as a mental trick. I'm grateful that he recommended it for this book.

Ask Stan to give the deck a shuffle. Take the cards back and say, "Stan, I could fan out the cards face up and ask you to think of a card, but you might feel that one card is more significant than the others. In other words, you might make a psychological choice." As you talk, hold the cards face up so that all can see the faces. Fan off a group of ten cards or so, saying, "You might think of one of these, for instance."

Place the group at the rear of the deck (on top if the deck were face down). Make sure you note the last card you fanned to, which is now the rearmost card (the top card if the deck were face down). You must remember this card. What's more, it must not be an obvious card, which the spectator might remember. The best choice would be a spot card. Let's say that the card you're remembering is the six of clubs.

You have just placed a packet to the rear of the face-up deck. "Or you might think of one of these . . ." Fan out five cards and place them at the rear of the deck, just as you did the previous group. ". . . or one of these . . ." Fan out five more cards and place them at the rear. ". . . or one of these." Fan out a significant number of cards, lift them off the deck, and then replace them onto the face-up deck. Close up the deck and turn it face down. Say: "So you could look through the deck and think of a card, but some cards might stand out. In fact, you may have seen a card that stood out from the others. Let's avoid that."

Hand Stan the deck. "Instead, I'd like you to think of a number . . . say, from one to ten. Got one? Okay, now please change your mind. Again, we want to make sure you don't make a psychological choice." Pause. "I'll turn away, and I'd like you to deal that many cards onto the table . . . very quietly. Now hide them somewhere; put them into your pocket or stick them under something."

When Stan finishes, turn back and take the balance of the deck. Count off ten cards from the top of the deck, taking them one *under* the other. In other words, the cards should retain their order.

Turn the packet face up. "Stan, I'm going to go through these cards. Please remember the card that lies at the number you thought of." (The card at that number will be the card you're remembering—in our example, the six of clubs.)

"Here, I'll deal them into your hand." He holds one of his hands out, palm up. Make it very obvious that you're averting your head, so that you can't see the cards as you deal. Slowly deal the face-up pile one card at a time onto Stan's palm, counting aloud as you do so.

When you're done, take the cards from Stan and place them face down on top of the deck. Have Stan cut the deck.

Hold the deck to your forehead and gradually reveal the name of the card: "I see clouds, dark clouds. Your card is black . . . I'd say it's a club. Think of the value. I'm starting to get it . . . Yes, it's rounded . . . maybe a nine. No, no . . . *like* a nine . . . It's a six. Your card is the six of clubs."

POWER OF THE MIND

Be Logical

I developed an interesting stunt based on an old logic conundrum. The result is sort of a cross between a trick and a puzzle. Regardless, it's good fun.

A study of the original puzzle will provide all you need to know about the basic principle involved in the stunt:

On a shelf are three boxes. Two black marbles are in one box. Two white marbles are in another box. And in a third box are a black marble and a white marble. The boxes are all labeled (Illus. 32).

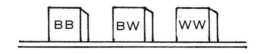

Illus. 32

One box is labeled BB, for black–black. Another is labeled WW for white–white. And the third is labeled BW for black–white. *No box*, however, is labeled correctly. The BB box, for instance, does not contain two black marbles.

The boxes are on a shelf that is above eye level. Your job is to figure out which box contains what marbles. You may reach up and remove a marble from any box. You may then repeat the procedure as many times as you wish. What is the least number of marbles you can remove and know *absolutely* what marbles are in each box?

Stop here if you want to think about it for a bit.

All right, here's the answer.

You remove exactly one marble. And you remove that marble from the box which is labeled BW. Suppose the color of that marble is white. What does this tell you?

It tells you that *both* marbles are white. The box cannot contain a black and a white marble because that would mean the box is labeled correctly. And the only other choice is two black marbles, and that, of course, is out of the question; one of the marbles is *white*!

What boxes remain? A box labeled BB and a box labeled WW. In one of those two boxes are two black marbles; which is it? It *must* be the box labeled WW. If the two black marbles are in the BB box, they would be correctly labeled, and that's against the rules.

To sum up: The box labeled BW contains two white marbles; the box labeled WW contains two black marbles; the box labeled BB must, therefore, contain a black marble and a white marble.

Suppose that the marble you initially remove from the BW box is black. You now know that the BW box contains two black marbles. The two white marbles can't be in the WW box, so they're in the BB box. And the WW box must contain a black marble and a white marble.

Fun? You bet. But let's take a look at my card stunt.

On the table, place a face-up red card, saying, "This is the marker card which marks the position of two red cards." Place two face-up red cards above the marker card, from your point of view. (Illus. 33 shows the *spectator's* point of view.)

Several inches to the left of your red marker card, place a face-up black card, saying, "This is the marker card which marks the position of the two black cards." Place two face-up black cards above the marker card.

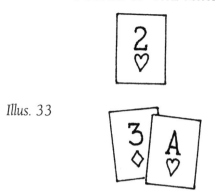

Illus. 33

In the middle, place any card face down, saying, "This is the card that marks the position of one card that is red and one that is black." The red card should be placed face up beneath the black card.

The entire layout, from the spectator's point of view, is shown in Illus. 34.

Illus. 34

Ask Les to help you out. "Your job, Les, should you choose to accept it, is to confuse me by moving these cards around. For instance, you might put the two black cards under the red marker." Move the two black cards over to illustrate the point. Place them back in their proper position. "Or you might decide to put the red and black combination under the black marker." Lift them up together and hold them under the black marker for a moment. Return them to their proper position.

"To make it even harder, make sure that no pair is under its proper marker. In other words, the two red cards can't be under the red marker. So, I'll turn my back, and you shift the pairs around face up. When you're satisfied, turn the pairs face down. And don't forget: No pair should be under its proper marker." When Les says he is ready, add this: "You might as well turn the marker cards face down also."

When Les is finished, you turn back to the group. Pick up the face-down card that originally marked the red and black combination and turn it face up. "Obviously, I know what this card is, so we'll use it as a divider." Drop the card face up on top of the cards above it (from your view). Pick up this three-card packet with your right hand and tap it edgewise onto the table, as though to even it up. Actually, you're sneaking a peek at the bottom card. All you need to know is whether the card is red or black, and you can get the color quite easily without looking directly at the card. Then place the three-card packet face down in your left hand.

The middle pair consists of either two reds or two blacks; you now know which it is. Let's assume that the two middle cards are blacks. Where are the reds? They *must* be under the black marker, for they *can't* be under the red marker. So you pick up the two cards under the black marker and place them face down on top on top of the three cards you're holding in your left hand.

You are now holding a pile of five cards. All are face down except the middle card—the so-called divider. The bottom two cards are black, and the top two are red.

On the table is another pair of face-down cards. The top one of these is red and the bottom one is black. Therefore, still keeping these cards face down, place the top card on top of those you're holding and place the bottom one on the bottom. You say, "And let's use the other two markers." In this instance, you put the red marker face down on top and the black marker face down on the bottom.

"Let's see if I correctly guessed where the blacks and reds are."

Deal out the top card of the packet (the red marker) face up. Deal the next three cards (reds) face up, overlapping them downward (Illus. 35). Take off the divider card and toss it aside face down. Deal the next four cards (blacks) into a separate pile face up, again overlapping downward. You did it perfectly.

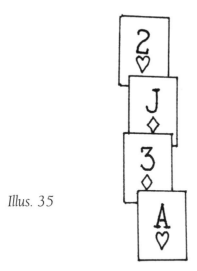

Illus. 35

Still, a review might help.

(1) When you turn back, pick up the face-down marker and place it face up on top of the two cards above it. Get a peek at

the bottom card of the three-card packet while tapping it on the table. Note the color of this card.

(2) Go to the marker of the same color. Take the two cards above this and place them, face down, on top of the packet in your hand.

(3) You now know the color of the bottom two cards in your hand. And you know that the top two cards in your hand are of the opposite color.

(4) A packet of two face-down cards remains on the table; one card is red and one is black. Place each one with its appropriate color in your packet; that is, place one face down on top and the other face down on the bottom.

(5) Two marker cards remain—one red and one black. Place each, still face down, with its appropriate group; that is, place one face down on top and the other face down on the bottom.

(6) Deal out a face-up pile consisting of four cards of the same color. Discard the face-up divider card. Deal out a separate face-up pile consisting of four cards, also of the same color (but, of course, different from the first four).

After a few trials, you'll find that the method is quite easy—almost automatic. The stunt may be repeated . . . once.

Be More Logical

The above is the original trick I developed based on the logical puzzle of the three boxes and the six marbles. Later, I came up with the following stunt which requires no sneakiness whatever.

The cards are laid out exactly as in "Be Logical." (Refer to Illus. 34.) You make the same proposal to a spectator: While your back is turned, he is to shift the pairs around so that no marker properly identifies a pair.

He then turns the pairs face down. Before you turn back, you add, "And you might as well turn the marker cards face down as well."

When you turn back, explain, "Despite the fact that you've mixed up these pairs, I'm going to try to pick these cards up in a certain order."

Stare at the cards for a moment, as though making up your mind. Then you indeed pick up the cards in a certain order. Here is the layout, using numbers rather than cards:

1	X	2
3	5	7
4	6	8

This is the spectator's view. It may be easier at this point in the stunt if you take a position beside the spectator as you collect the cards.

The marker cards are 1, X, and 2. You start by pushing the middle marker, X, aside, saying, "We'll need an even number of cards."

Pick up the marker card on the right (2) and place it on top of Pile 3–4 (the pile on the left). Pick up this three-card pile.

Go to Pile 7–8 (the pile on the right). Pick off the top card of this pile (7) and place it on top of the group you're holding. Pick up the other card that made up this pair (8) and place it on the bottom of those you're holding. From top to bottom you're now holding five cards in this order: 7, 2, 3, 4, 8.

Remaining to be picked up are the pair in the middle (Pile 5–6) and the marker card on the left (1).

Take the top card from the middle pile (5) and place it on top of those you're holding. Place the marker card (1) on top of those you're holding. Finally, place the other card in the middle (6) on top of those in your hand.

From top to bottom, the pile now runs 6, 1, 5, 7, 2, 3, 4, 8. After practicing the pickup procedure a few times, you'll find that it's actually quite simple.

Now the pile you're holding either alternates blacks and reds, starting with a black card, or it contains four red cards in a row, followed by four black cards.

Possibility 1

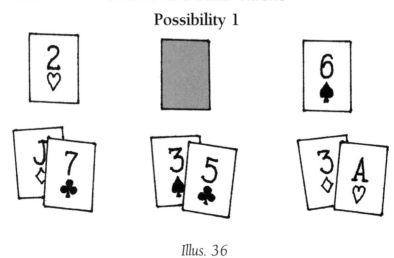

Illus. 36

"Let's see how I did."

Turn the top card of the pile face up. If it's a black card, immediately deal the next card face up to the right of it. Continue by dealing the next card face up on top of the first card, overlapping it downward so that all can see that both cards are black. Deal the fourth card face up on top of the card on the right, again overlapping downward. Continue alternating until you have a pile of four black cards on the left and a pile of four red cards on the right.

Suppose you turn over the top card of your pile and it's red. Deal the card face up on the table. Deal the next card face up on top of this, overlapping downward. Deal two more cards in this way. All the reds are in a face-up pile on the table. To the right of this pile, deal out the four remaining cards into the same kind of pile. You have managed to separate the reds and blacks.

How is this possible? When the rules are followed, there are only two possible layouts the spectator can end up with (Illus. 36 and 37).

You pick up the cards in such a manner that either layout is accommodated.

Possibility 2

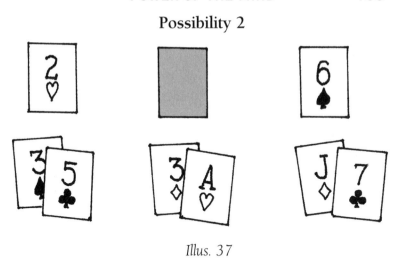

Illus. 37

If you're going to repeat the trick, start by explaining, "Let's try again. This time, you can mix the pairs the same way as you did the first time or try it a different way—your choice. Regardless, we'll make it a little different this time."

That last sentence is most important. Chances are, the spectator will mix the pairs in the only other way possible. If he does, the conclusion will be different. If the conclusion is the same, and the spectator questions you on it, simply say, "Didn't you notice how I picked up the cards differently?"

You can, in fact, pick them up differently. You can devise your own variation or simply pick them up *faster*.

Note

Here is another way of picking up the cards which produces the same result as the method given above, except that the position of the reds and blacks is reversed. The layout is this, after you've discarded the middle marker card:

1		2
3	5	7
4	6	8

As before, numbers 1 and 2 are the marker cards. Place 1 under Pile 7–8.

Pick up the three-card pile.

Place 3 on the bottom of the pile. Place 4 on top of the pile. Place 5 on top. Place 2 on top. Place 6 on top.

Simple Logic

There is a truly ancient coin trick which a few magicians have converted into a mental demonstration with cards. The versions I've seen required considerable memory work. In my version, I have simplified the mental labor—for me, as much as for my readers.

Ask for the help of three women. Hand the deck to one and ask that it be shuffled. Ask another of the volunteers to remove from the deck any ace, two, and three. These are tossed face up onto the table. You take the deck back. "In a moment, each of you will take one of these three cards. My back will be turned, so I'll have no way of knowing who has what card. But first, we'll need more cards. Let's use ten cards."

Deal ten cards into a pile. Pause in thought for a moment. "Wait a minute. We already have three cards. If we add 10 to that, the number becomes 13. And 13 is bad luck. Just to be on the safe side, we'll use the lucky number seven."

Deal seven more cards on top of your pile of ten. Again pause in thought. "Thirteen is a powerful number. We'd better have another seven." Deal seven more cards into the pile.

The pile now consists of 24 cards. And three cards—ace, two, and three—are face up on the table.

Put the rest of the deck into your pocket. Or at least move it out of everyone else's reach. Pick up the pile of 24 cards.

The three volunteers are standing in front of you. Count them aloud from left to right: "One, two, three." Nod your head. Point to Spectator 1, saying, "So you get one card." Hand her one card.

Point to Spectator 2, saying, "And you get two cards." Hand her two cards.

Point to Spectator 3, saying, "And, of course, you get three cards." Hand her three cards. Set the rest of the cards face down onto the table within easy reach of your volunteers.

Turn your back and say, "There's an ace, a two, and a three on the table. Each of you take one of them, please. It doesn't matter who gets which one. The idea is to fool me." Pause. "Now we must establish a relationship between the three selected cards and the remaining pile on the table. Will the person who has the ace please take the same number of cards as I gave you. For example, if I gave you two cards, take two more cards from the pile."

Pause. "Will the person who has the two please take *twice* the number of cards as I gave you. For example, if I gave you two cards, take four cards from the pile."

Pause. "Will the person who has the three please take *four times* the number of cards as I gave you. For example, if I gave you two cards, take eight cards from the pile."

Pause. "Everyone, please, hide your cards–both the one you chose and the cards you took from the pile."

When everyone is done, turn back to the group. Left on the table are one, two, three, five, six, or seven cards. (Four cards cannot be left, unless someone erred.) If more than one card is on the table, spread the cards out, saying, "Were there enough cards?" (Actually, you mentally count the number of cards. Remember that number!)

You are assured that the number of cards was sufficient. "Good."

If you plan on repeating the trick, push the remaining card or cards aside. Otherwise, pick up the rest of the deck (or remove it from your pocket) and toss it onto the card or cards on the table.

This number that you're remembering tells you precisely who has what card. Here is a chart, based on the number of cards left on the table:

Spectators	1	2	3
1 card left:	A	2	3
2 cards left:	2	A	3
3 cards left:	A	3	2
5 cards left:	2	3	A
6 cards left:	3	A	2
7 cards left:	3	2	A

Looking at the chart, you can see that if two cards are left on the table, Spectator 1 has the two, Spectator 2 has the ace, and Spectator 3 has the three. Your job is to stare at each spectator in turn and then tell each one what her card is.

I have divided the above chart into two sections so that you can note that the bottom section is identical to the top section, except that it is reversed and upside-down. Study the chart for a moment. Do you notice, for instance, that in the middle column we see **2 A 3** in the top section and, the reverse, **3 A 2** in the bottom section? Furthermore, in the right column of the upper section, we see **3 3 2**, while in the left lower column, we see the reverse, **2 3 3**.

Do you have the chart memorized yet? Me neither. Let's simplify the chart. After all, it's only necessary that you know what Spectators 1 and 2 hold. Obviously, Spectator 3 must hold the missing card. So here's the system:

You must think of the number of cards left on the table as two trios: **1, 2, 3** and **5, 6, 7**.

1, 2, or 3 Cards Left on the Table

Start by finding out what Spectator 2 holds. If the number left on the table is three, Spectator 2 holds the three. Otherwise, subtract the number on the table from three.

If the result is one, Spectator 2 holds the ace.

If the result is two, Spectator 2 holds the two.

Spectator 1 then holds the lowest card possible.

Spectator 3 holds the remaining card.

Let me explain further. First, try to figure out what Spectator 2 holds.

If three cards are left on the table, Spectator 2 holds the three.

If one or two cards are left on the table, subtract that number from three. If one card is on the table, subtract one from three, getting two, so Spectator 2 holds the two.

If two cards are left on the table, subtract two from three, getting one (ace), so Spectator 2 holds the ace.

How about Spectator 1? *Spectator 1 holds the lowest card possible.* If Spectator 2 holds the ace (one), the lowest card possible is two. So Spectator 1 must hold the two.

If Spectator 2 holds the two, the lowest card possible is one. So Spectator 1 must hold the ace.

If Spectator 2 holds the three, again the lowest card possible is one. So Spectator 1 must hold the ace.

You now know Spectator 2's card and Spectator 1's card. Clearly, Spectator 3 holds the remaining card.

5, 6, or 7 Cards Left on the Table

If you understand the above, you should have no trouble with this. It's exactly the same, except in two respects:

(1) Before applying the rules, you subtract the number of cards left from eight. You then begin the regular procedure. If three is the result of the subtraction, then Spectator 2's card is a three. If one or two is the result of the subtraction, then you must subtract that number from three.

(2) After you determine what Spectator 2 is holding, Spectator 1 is holding the *highest* possible number, instead of the lowest.

As before, you must start by discovering what card Spectator 2 is holding.

Five cards are left on the table. Subtract five from eight, getting three. So Spectator 2 holds the three. What does Spectator

1 hold? Spectator 1 holds the *highest* possible number. In this instance, then, she holds the two. Since Spectator 2 holds the three and Spectator 1 holds the two, Spectator 3 must hold the ace.

Six cards are left on the table. Subtract six from eight, getting two. As above, the two must be subtracted from three, giving you one, or ace. So Spectator 2 holds the ace. Spectator 1 holds the highest possible number; in this instance, that's three. So Spectator 1 holds the three. Clearly, Spectator 3 holds the two.

Seven cards are left on the table. Subtract seven from eight, getting one. Then, subtract one from three, getting two. So Spectator 2 holds the two. The highest possible number that Spectator 1 can hold is three. So Spectator 1 holds the three. And, by elimination, Spectator 3 holds the ace.

Review

(1) Get three volunteers. Have one of them shuffle the deck. Have another remove from the deck any ace, two, and three.

(2) Say that you'll use ten cards. Deal ten into a pile. Realize suddenly that, combined with the other three cards, this makes 13. Deal seven more cards onto the pile. Then, to be on the safe side, deal seven more cards onto the pile. Set the rest of the deck aside or put it into your pocket.

(3) Give one card to Spectator 1, two cards to Spectator 2, and three cards to Spectator 3. Set the rest of the packet near your volunteers.

(4) Turn your back. Each volunteer takes either the ace, two, or three.

(5) The person with the ace takes the same number of cards as you gave her.

(6) The person with the two takes twice the number of cards that you gave her.

(7) The person with the three takes four times the number of cards that you gave her.

(8) Each volunteer hides all her cards. You turn back and count the cards remaining on the table.

(9) If the number of cards left on the table is three, Spectator 2 holds the three. If the number is one or two, subtract that number from three to get the value of Spectator 2's card. Spectator 1 holds the lowest number possible.

(10) If the number of cards left on the table is five, six, or seven, you then follow (9) with these exceptions:

(A) Before applying the rules, you subtract the number of cards left from eight.

(B) After you determine what Spectator 2 is holding, Spectator 1 is holding the *highest* possible number, instead of the lowest.

I Think I Can

This is my somewhat simplified version of a trick called "Think in Synch," which appeared in the book *Card Craft* by J.K. Hartman. The basic idea is quite familiar to magicians: A spectator thinks of one of a number of cards. The magician shows the spectator several groups of cards, asking the spectator to identify in which one his card lies. Actually, each group of cards contains just one of the original cards shown, and the magician knows where in the group that card lies.

Start by asking Ward to help out. Turn the deck face up and say to Ward, "In a moment I'm going to ask you to think of one of these cards. But right now, I'd like you to keep your mind perfectly clear." As you speak, note the name of the bottom card, the card at the face of the deck, and remember it. Let's say this card is the six of spades. Fan cards into your right hand, casually showing them. Actually, you mentally count 12 cards. Place these on top of the deck. Turn the deck face down. Your key card, the six of spades, is now twelfth from the top.

"Ward, I'd like you to think of one of these cards."

Lift off the top card of the deck and hold it up so that Ward can see its face. Take your time; let Ward get a good look. Return to the deck and take the next card *in front of* the first card. Hold the two cards up so that Ward can see only the face of the card you just took off the deck. Continue, showing in turn the faces of the third, fourth, and fifth cards from the top. As you show the cards at a deliberate pace, mentally count them.

After showing five cards, lower the packet of five but don't place it on top of the deck. Ask Ward: "Do you have a card?" He probably does. But if he doesn't, place the packet of five on the bottom of the deck. Then show Ward the next five cards precisely as you showed him the first five. He probably has a card by now. (In a note at the end of the trick, I explain what to do if he hasn't chosen a card at this point.)

Replace the five cards on top of the deck. Have Ward, or anyone else, give the deck a complete cut. And the deck may be given a few more complete cuts.

"Your thought-of card is lost in the deck, Ward. But I'm going to find it."

Fan through the deck, faces toward yourself, looking for your key card. Let's assume that Ward chose a card from the first five cards. When you find your key card, the six of spades, start counting with that card, mentally saying, "One." Count an additional number for each card until you count card number seven. Cut the deck so that the seventh card you counted becomes the top card of the deck. On the bottom of the deck are the five cards that Ward chose from.

What if Ward chose a card from the second group of five cards? This time, when you find your key card, count it as one. Count the next card as two. Cut the deck so that the second card you counted becomes the top card of the deck. Again, on the bottom are the five cards that Ward chose from.

Turn the deck face down. "Sorry, Ward, this is too big a task, even for me. I'll have to choose from a smaller number of cards."

Make a quarter turn to the right so that your left side is more toward the group. Ask Ward to hold out one of his hands, palm up. Take the deck in the over-hand shuffle position. Begin the shuffle by drawing off into the left hand four cards. With your left hand, place these four face down onto Ward's hand. "Here are some cards." Pause briefly.

"I'd better give you some more." Now you'll see why you made that quarter turn to the right. You don't want anyone to see your next sneaky move as you once more over-hand shuffle. With the left fingers and thumb, draw off together the top card and bottom card of the deck. These are easily taken together by squeezing the left fingers and thumb together as you raise the rest of the deck with your right hand.

As you do this, mentally count, "One."

Continue by drawing off single cards on top of the first two. When you reach the count of four, stop shuffling. You now hold five cards in your hand, and the bottom card of these is one of the five that Ward looked at. With your left hand place these five cards face down on top of the others Ward is holding. He now holds nine cards, and the fifth from the top is one of the cards that he looked at.

Set the rest of the deck aside.

Say to Ward, "Fan through those cards and see if your card is in that group."

Avert your head while he does so. If he doesn't see his card, take the packet back and set it aside.

Repeat the shuffling procedure and hand Ward another packet, saying, "Try this bunch, Ward."

Continue until Ward sees his card in one of the groups of nine. Have him continue to hold that packet.

"Here's what I'd like you to do in a moment: Take off the top card of the packet and hold it up so that you can see its face, but I can't. When you're done, place the card on the bottom of the packet. And then do the same thing with the next card. But beware! I'll be watching you carefully, so try not to give away the fact that you're looking at your card. Still, I think I'll be able to tell. You can go ahead now."

Ward looks at a card for a moment and then places it on the bottom. You mentally count, "One."

You continue counting until he's looking at the fifth card. Pause very briefly and then say, "Ward, you're looking at the card you thought of."

Review

(1) Get Ward to help out.

(2) Turn the deck face up. Note the bottom card, your key card. Casually fan through the cards, showing them. Actually, you count to the twelfth card from the bottom. Cut the cards at this point. Your key card is now twelfth from the top.

(3) Tell Ward, "I'd like you to think of one of these cards." Show him the top five cards of the deck one at a time, keeping the cards in their original order. Ask him if he's thought of one. If not, put the five cards on the bottom and show Ward the next five cards. Ask if he has chosen one. He probably has.

(4) After Ward has chosen a card, place the five cards on top of the deck. The deck should be given one or more complete cuts.

(5) Fan through the face-up deck, looking for your key card.

(a) If Ward chose a card from the first group you showed him, start counting with the key card and stop counting with card number seven. Cut the deck so that card number seven becomes the top card of the deck. On the bottom are the five cards Ward chose from.

(b) If Ward chose a card from the second group, count the key card as one and the next card as two. Cut the deck so that card number two becomes the top card of the deck. On the bottom are the five cards Ward chose from.

(6) Tell Ward it's too tough and you'll have to work with a smaller number of cards. Ask him to hold out his hand, palm up. Make a quarter turn to the right in preparation for an over-hand shuffle. Shuffle off four cards one at a time into the left hand. Place these face down onto Ward's hand. Restarting the over-hand shuffle, draw off the top and bottom cards together in the first move. Draw off three more cards on top of these two. Place this packet of five face down on top of the other

cards in Ward's hand.

(7) Ask Ward to fan through the cards to see if his is there. If not, set that packet aside. Give Ward another packet of nine as described above. Continue until he sees his card in a packet.

(8) Tell Ward to hold the packet face down and look at each card separately, starting with the top card. If the card is not his, he is to place it on the bottom. When he reaches the fifth card, you tell him that he's looking at the card he thought of.

Note

Suppose that Ward has still not chosen his card after you've shown him two groups of five. Place the second group of five on the bottom of the deck. Take off the next two cards together and fan them out so that Ward can see them both. "Think of one of these two cards, Ward." Replace them on top of the deck. The lowermost of the two cards is your key card, the nine of spades.

Have the deck cut a few times. Fan through the deck, faces toward yourself. Cut the cards so that your key card, the nine of spades, becomes the top card of the deck. Set the deck face down onto the table. The nine of spades is on top, and the other possible selection is now the bottom card. Ask Ward to name his card. If he names the nine of spades, you turn it up on top. If he names a different card, you turn the deck face up on the table, showing the bottom card.

Sometimes a spectator will refuse to name his card. "*You* tell me; *you're* the magician." Ah, if only you knew Karate! But there's hope. Say, "You've got me. I have no idea of what card you took. I really hate failing, but there you are. So what *was* the card you thought of?" Most spectators will now name the card. Then you say, "I lied. I had your card all the time." You show it on the top or bottom.

But maybe the spectator won't fall for this and *still* refuses to name the card. Laugh knowingly. "Admit it . . . you forgot it, right?" This ought to work. Actually, I've never had to go quite that far.

MIND-BOGGLING FUN

All but one of the items in this section are quite wacky. If you're performing your mental tricks with a twinkle in your eye, you can readily toss in some of these. But if you're presenting yourself as a serious mentalist, you'd naturally want to avoid such silliness.

Whether you're doing mental tricks or not, you might include a few of these. They provide a snappy bit of humor, a little break from the more thoughtful tricks.

A Little Error

This is the only one of the group that is a genuine trick. The basic principle has been used in quite a few tricks. My application is both deceptive and amusing.

You'll need the assistance of two spectators. Beth and Randy seem particularly eager, so you choose them. No matter how bright Beth and Randy are, they might have trouble with your directions, so it's best to start things off with a demonstration.

"Here's what I'm going to ask you to do. Beth, I'm going to ask you to shuffle the deck and then deal as many cards as you wish into two equal piles."

As you explain, shuffle the deck, and deal out two equal piles of at least ten cards each.

"You keep one pile, Beth, and push the other one over to Randy."

"Each of you will cut off some cards from your pile." Indicate that they should do so.

"Then you'll look at the bottom card of those you've cut off. That'll be your chosen card." It's best at this point that they do *not* look at their bottom card; you don't want them to confuse that card with the one they'll choose in a moment.

"Beth, you'll place the pile you cut off on top of the pile that Randy has on the table." Take the pile from her and place it on top of Randy's pile on the table. "And Randy, you'll place the cards you cut off on top of Beth's pile on the table." Take the cards he's holding and place them on top of Beth's pile on the table.

"Put the piles together by putting either pile on top." Demonstrate. "And then each of you gives the combined pile a complete cut." Have them do so.

Hand the cards to Beth. "Don't worry if you don't remember it all. I'll talk you through it. Start by shuffling the deck and then dealing out two equal piles onto the table." When she deals the cards down, you keep silent count of the number that goes into one of the piles. Let's assume that she deals two piles of nine cards each. *Remember this number.*

Turn your back and continue your directions: "Beth, place one of the piles in front of you, and push one of them in front of Randy. Now I'd like each of you to shuffle your pile and put it back onto the table." Pause. "Each of you please cut off some cards from your pile and look at the bottom card of those you cut off. Remember that card, because later I'm going to read your mind and tell you exactly what that card is. Are you still holding your cut-off pile, Beth?" Yes, she is. "Did you look at the bottom card?" She did. "All right. Place that pile on top of the cards that Randy left on the table." Pause briefly.

"Randy, are you still holding your cut-off pile?" Yes, he is. "Will you remember the bottom card of that pile?" Yes, he will. "Can you guess where I want you to place that pile? That's right. Please put it on top of the cards that Beth left on the table."

After another brief pause, continue: "Beth, please put one pile on top of the other; it doesn't matter which goes on top."

Turn back to the group. "Randy, please give the pile a complete cut." When he finishes, say, "Beth, I'd like you to cut the cards also."

After she's done, pick up the packet, saying, "Eventually, I'm going to reveal the names of both your cards. But I'll start with Beth. Please concentrate on your card, Beth, as I look at the faces of these cards."

Fan through the cards, faces toward you. After a moment, say, "Are you concentrating, Beth? I'm not getting it. Just think of the suit of your card." Fan through again. "No, it's not working. Instead, Beth, just think of the . . . of the . . ." Your eyes light up. With a snap of your fingers, you say, "I've got it! I've got it! Just think of the *value* of your card."

Go through the cards again, rather half-heartedly this time. "No, I just can't get it, Beth. What's the name of your card?"

She names the card; let's suppose it's the four of diamonds. You remember that in the beginning nine cards were in each pile. Again, you fan through the cards, faces toward you. When you get to the four of diamonds, start counting with the *next card*. Count to nine, the number of cards that were in each pile. (If you run out of cards before you complete the count, simply continue counting with the card at the face of the packet.) The card that you land on is the other chosen card. Let's say this is the six of spades. Without letting anyone see its face, remove it from the packet and place it face down onto the table. As you do this, you demonstrate that you're full of confidence again. "All right, one down and one to go." (It's important that you say this. Without making a big deal of it, you strongly imply that you've just placed the four of diamonds onto the table.)

"Randy, please concentrate on your card." Extend the probing process with Randy for a brief time; unfortunately, you're still unsuccessful. Then you say, "I've got it! I knew I'd get it." Brief pause. "Yes, a *headache* is what I've got." Pause for the laugh or, of course, the wide-eyed stares. "Okay, Randy, what's your card?"

"Six of spades," he says.

"No wonder I couldn't get your card. I really goofed up. I put the wrong card onto the table."

Turn the card on the table over. The six of spades.

It may take the group several seconds to figure out that you've done something quite magical.

A Marked Card

Hand a deck of cards to Cindy, asking her to shuffle thoroughly. Hand her a pen and then turn your back. "I would like you to select any card you wish and put your initials on its face for later identification. When the ink is dry, put the card back into the deck and shuffle."

Turn back and take the deck. Rapidly fan through the cards and remove the initialed card. Hold it out to Cindy, saying, "And here we have your freely selected card. Just another one of my miracles."

Many will be amazed at first. Gradually, all will be amused as they realize that you picked out the only card with initials on it.

Card Reading

Let's try that extreme rarity, a card trick without cards. Wally Wilson loves performing this one.

Ask Rhea to think of any card in the deck, any card at all. "Do you have one?" She does. "Please concentrate on that card while I write down my prediction."

Remove a slip of paper from your pocket. Write on it: *Yes, that's my card.*

Give the paper one inward fold so that the writing is concealed. On one of the exposed sides, write this: *No.*

Give the paper another inward fold and hand it to Rhea.

"Tell me, Rhea, do you think I know the card you're thinking of?" If she doesn't say no, you might have to persist. For instance, she might say, "I don't know," or, "I'm not sure." You might say, "Be honest, Rhea. Do you think I know?"

If she still dallies, you might force the issue: "Do I know the card or not, Rhea? Yes or no?"

If the answer is yes, you've chosen the wrong spectator. But you still have an out. Ask the rest of the group: "What do *you* think? Yes or no?" The answer will always be no. In any event, you'll always have a few "no" answers, and that's enough to work with.

"So the answer is no. Please unfold the paper once, Rhea, and read my prediction aloud."

Make sure she doesn't unfold the paper all the way. She reads the prediction. You correctly predicted that the answer would be no. What an all-star!

"Let's find out if I correctly predicted your card. Open the paper the rest of the way, Rhea, and read what's there."

She reads, "Yes, that's my card."

People generally catch on quickly that she's reading precisely what you've written, and they're amused.

But Wally Wilson adds a special touch that is all his own. He pauses to give everyone a chance to catch on. Then he says to his assistant, "Could you read that with a bit more feeling."

Strange Transmission

It's time to test Louise's ESP. "Louise, I'd like to try a feat of telepathy with you. I'm going to concentrate on one card in the deck. It won't be a face card, and it won't be an ace. I'd like you to concentrate also."

Both of you strain your brains. "Are you getting a card, Louise?" She is. "What is it?" She names it.

"I can't believe it! That's *exactly* the right card. Let's try it again."

More than likely, she won't be interested in doing it again. If she is, however, give it another shot. She can't miss!

Name That Card!

Since Louise has been such a good sport, the least you can do is reciprocate by letting her think of a card. This is another weird notion that I came up with many moons ago.

"Louise, I believe that I can name any card you think of. Please think of a card, any card at all. And I will name it."

You both concentrate. "I'll now name your card. I've decided to name your card . . . Benjamin." Pause. "Go ahead. Think of another card, and I'll name it."

The Name Is Familiar

Since devising this silly stunt some years ago, I've had a lot of fun with it. Perhaps you will, too.

Ron is open-minded on the subject of ESP, so he would be the perfect subject. "Ron, I'd like you to fix a playing card in your mind. It can be an ace, a face card, a spot card—it doesn't matter. Do you have one? Please concentrate on it. I, myself, will concentrate fiercely. In less than a minute, I will name aloud the very card you're thinking of. Ready?"

You rapidly name every card in the deck. Start with clubs, for instance. Call out, "Ace of clubs, king of clubs, queen of clubs, jack of clubs, ten of clubs," etc. Go all the way down to the two of clubs, and then do the hearts, the spades, and the diamonds. And don't forget the joker.

When making the proposition, be sure to say "playing card," rather than just "card." I performed this once for a woman, asking her to think of "any card." When I finished, she said, "Wrong!"

"How can I be wrong?" I asked.

"I was thinking of my credit card."

I suppose she could equally well have been thinking of her library card.

THE THREATENING KINGS

It's high time that you learned the best known setup in card magic. Let's deal with the values first. From the top, the cards run

8 K 3 10 2 7 9 5 Q 4 A 6 J

It's easy to remember; just memorize this sentence: Eight kings threatened to save ninety-five queens for one sick knave.

Eight (8) - kings (K) - threa (3) - tened (10) - to (2) - save (7) - ninety (9) - five (5) - queens (Q) - for (4) - one (A) - sick (6) - knave (J).

One of the common uses of the setup is to stack the entire deck.

The values are as given above, and the suits are set up in a repeated order of clubs, hearts, spades, diamonds (CHaSeD). So from top to bottom, the deck would be in this order:

8C KH 3S 10D 2C 7H 9S 5D QC 4H AS 6D JC

8H KS 3D 10C 2H 7S 9D 5C QH 4S AD 6C JH

8S KD 3C 10H 2S 7D 9C 5H QS 4D AC 6H JS

8D KC 3H 10S 2D 7C 9H 5S QD 4C AH 6S JD

Obviously, a deck set up like this cannot be shuffled. It can, however, be given complete cuts without destroying the basic order. And, after you've done several tricks using the setup deck, you can indeed shuffle the cards and proceed to perform tricks that don't require a setup.

In each of the following items, the basic trick is the same: A spectator looks at a card, and you read his mind. The way you discover his card is by learning the name of the card above it in the sequence. For instance, you learn that the card above the chosen card is the queen of spades. You know that following a queen is a four. You also know that following a spade is a diamond. The selected card, therefore, is the four of diamonds.

Cut and Peek – 1

Have Nancy cut the deck a few times. After another cut, have her take the top card. Pick up the deck and, as you talk about how difficult it is to read someone's mind, casually sneak a peek at the bottom card. The chosen card is the one that follows this in sequence.

Suppose you see that the bottom card is the nine of clubs. In the sequence, a five always follows a nine. And a heart always follows a club. Therefore, the selected card is the five of hearts. After announcing this fact, you can take the card back and place it on top. You're ready for a repeat. Or you might try something slightly more sophisticated, like the next trick.

Cut and Peek – 2

Fan out the deck for Nancy to select a card. Cut the cards at the point at which she removes the card. Again, sneak a look at the bottom card. The selected card will be the one that follows it in sequence.

Sneaky Peek – 1

How about arranging it so that the spectator actually *shows* you the card that appears before the chosen one in the sequence? This particularly clever method by Tom Frame accomplishes just that.

Since Warren has graciously agreed to help you, hand him the deck, saying, "Please hold the cards behind your back." Then, with appropriate pauses, continue: "Now cut off some cards from the top of the deck and put them onto the table. Take the next card from the top of the deck and, without looking at it or letting me see it, slip it into your pocket."

Warren does all this perfectly.

"Now please place the rest of the deck on top of the cards on the table."

Once more, he accomplishes the feat.

"Warren, neither of us knows your card, right? Do you think you could figure out which one is missing by fanning through the cards? Why don't you pick up the deck and give it a try."

He picks up the deck, turns it over, and starts fanning through the cards. In the process, *you* see the bottom card. So the missing card must be the next card in sequence. After several seconds, stop him, saying, "Warren, I think this is going to be nearly impossible . . . even for you."

Indicate that he is to set the deck down. "But we have hope. Perhaps I, with all my semi-mystical powers, can determine the name of the card." Concentrate fiercely and name the card.

Ask Warren to remove the card from his pocket and show it to all. What do you know! You're right again. Toss the card on top, and the deck is set up for more miracles.

Sneaky Peek – 2

This last method is of my own devising. Sharon, who has agreed to assist you, is holding the deck. You turn your back and say, "Sharon, please hold the cards face down. Now please very quietly deal off cards into a *face-up* pile." Don't say anything for several seconds so that Sharon can get started. "When you finally deal out a card that you like, just stop dealing. Remember that card and put it aside face down."

Wait until Sharon says she's done. Turn around, quickly noting the top card of the ones she dealt onto the table. Look away, as you begin concentrating. Casually gesture toward the face-up cards as you comment, "Oh, would you turn those face down please." Clearly these will interfere with your enormous divination powers. But it's all right; you name the correct card.

The chosen card goes on top of the bottom portion of the deck. The dealt-off cards go on top, and the sequence is restored.

Something Is Missing

You can tell a card by knowing the one above or below it in the setup. You can also easily tell when a card is missing from the setup. Here are two simple ways to utilize the latter.

(1) Have someone think of a card and then fan through the cards and remove it from the deck. You explain, "I'm so attuned to the deck that I'm absolutely certain I can fan through and discover what card is missing." No one believes you, of course. But, for a change, you're actually telling the truth. Fan through and notice which card is missing from the setup. Close up the cards.

"It's not working. Maybe we should try telepathy. Please concentrate on the color of your card." Continue in this manner until you divine the selected card.

(2) Ask someone to think of a card, remove it from the deck, and stare at its face as he concentrates. You, of course, concentrate also.

"I'm starting to get it, I think."

Have him place the card on top of the deck and then give the cards a complete cut or two.

"Please continue to concentrate on your card. I'll see if I can find it."

Of course you can. You fan through and find the card that's out of sequence.

If you want to restore the setup, remove the selected card and place it face down onto the table. "I'm not quite sure. Let's see . . ."

Fan through until you come to the broken sequence from which the chosen card came. Cut the cards at this point. Pause a moment. "No, I guess I was right the first time. What's the name of your card."

The card is named and you turn it over. You then turn it face down and put it on top of the deck. The setup is restored.

Television Mentalism

Years ago, I was watching television late one night with two of my older children. A famous mentalist was on the panel. He had a deck of cards cut a number of times. Then he fanned the cards out face down before another member of the panel, a singer, and asked him to remove a group of cards from the middle.

The singer did so. After deliberating for a moment, the mentalist haltingly named all the cards in the group withdrawn by the singer. Each time the mentalist named a card, the singer handed it to him. When the mentalist got about a third of the way through, I began naming each card just before he did. Thus, I became a hero—however briefly—in the eyes of some of my offspring.

What did the mentalist do? He cut the cards at the point at which the singer withdrew his cards. Then he sneaked a peek at the bottom card. With great effort, he began naming cards. I can't remember exactly which ones, but it went something like this: "Four of hearts, ace of spades, six of diamonds, jack of clubs, eight of hearts . . ." At this point, I was able to precede him with each card: "King of spades, three of diamonds, ten of clubs." And so on.

Clearly the deck was set up in the "eight kings" order. Once the mentalist saw the bottom card, he knew the next card in the setup and, of course, every card after that.

A Little Extra Help

Here we have a Charles W. Simon idea that can involve as many as seven spectators. What audience participation!

You tell the group, "I'll need seven volunteers. One will select a card from the deck. Others will take part in choosing a number at random from the phone book. One volunteer will dial the number, another will speak on the phone. If all of us really concentrate, I believe that this perfect stranger will be able to name the selected card. Let's find out."

Naturally, the deck is set up in the "eight kings" order. You ask for seven volunteers. Spectator 7, who hangs back a bit, is your confederate.

Spectator 1 cuts the deck and takes the top card. You pick up the deck and, as you patter about what is going to happen, you make sure that Spectator 7 gets a look at the bottom card. Since he is familiar with the setup, he now knows the name of the selected card. Let's say the chosen card is the nine of clubs.

Spectator 2 opens the phone book to any page. Spectator 3 chooses either the left or the right page. Spectator 4 picks a column on that page. Spectator 5 picks a line. Spectator 6 dials the number. As he dials, you tell Spectator 7, "Ask for the name of the chosen card."

As soon as Spectator 6 finishes dialing, Spectator 7 takes the phone. After a few seconds, he says, "Can you tell me the name of the chosen card?" He pauses a second and then hangs up.

"Was it a man or a woman?" you ask.

"A woman."

"What did she say?"

"She said it was the nine of clubs."

You turn to Spectator 1. "And what is your card?"

Miracle of miracles! It *is* the nine of clubs.

Notes

(1) Naturally, you don't want to annoy perfect strangers any more than you absolutely have to. If your confederate acts promptly, the whole routine can be accomplished before the phone is answered. Anyway, in this electronic age, often as not you get an answering machine.

(2) Clearly the trick may be performed with fewer than seven volunteers. I have done it with as few as three helpers. Just make sure that your confederate is the one who talks on the phone.

(3) The trick can actually be performed without a setup deck, but it isn't as strong. The deck is spread out face up and a spectator touches one of the cards. Obviously, everyone knows which card is chosen. Your confederate, when speaking on the phone, asks what the card is, pauses, and then says, "She said it's the nine of clubs," naming the card.

MASTERY LEVELS
CHART & INDEX